Joy in Disguise

Joy in Disguise

Meeting Jesus in the Dark Times

Edward S. Little

Morehouse Publishing

An imprint of Church Publishing Incorporated
Harrisburg–New York

Morehouse Publishing, 4775 Linglestown Road, Harrisburg, PA 17112

Morehouse Publishing, 445 Fifth Avenue, New York, NY 10016

Morehouse Publishing is an imprint of Church Publishing Incorporated.

Cover design by Laurie Klein Westhafer
Interior design by Scribe

Library of Congress Cataloging-in-Publication Data

Little, Edward S., 1947–
  Joy in disguise : meeting Jesus in the dark times / Edward S. Little II.
    p. cm.
  Includes bibliographical references (p.).
  ISBN 978-0-8192-2328-9 (pbk.)
  1. Bible. N.T. Philippians—Criticism, interpretation, etc. 2. Joy—Biblical teaching. I. Title.
BS2705.6.J6L58 2009
227'.606–dc22   2008038811

Printed in the United States of America

08 09 10 11 12 13   10 9 8 7 6 5 4 3 2 1

CONTENTS

A PERSONAL NOTE

At first glance, writing appears to be a supremely solitary occupation. The author sits at a desk, and words make their way from brain to fingers to keys to a computer screen. Silence and isolation are prerequisites of the task. Distractions must be minimized, people kept at a distance, and other concerns set aside for the sake of unimpaired creativity.

I have come to realize, however, that the reality is rather different. To begin with, this book could never have been written without the generosity of the Diocese of Northern Indiana. The diocese provided a three-month sabbatical leave—and, thus, the time and the space to transform outlines on a yellow pad into prose—but above all prayer, encouragement, and a loving and supportive Christian community. I praise God every day for the gift of my brothers and sisters in the diocese and for the privilege of serving as their bishop, friend, and fellow pilgrim.

This book began its life as a retreat given at the DeKoven Center in Racine, Wisconsin. Later, the outlines were edited and refined as I offered these reflections at clergy conferences in the dioceses of Fond du Lac and Western Louisiana. Many of the ideas, stories, and teachings were "test-marketed" in the parishes of the Diocese of Northern Indiana in the course of Sunday visitations. At each stage, the Christian community provided a setting where I could think through the implications of St. Paul's Letter to the Philippians in company with a band of disciples and friends.

I am grateful to the monks of St. Gregory's Abbey in Three Rivers, Michigan, where I spent a week expanding the outlines and writing the initial material for the book. I am so very grateful as well to Dr. Fred and Pam Harris, members of St. Andrew's Parish in Valparaiso, Indiana, who offered the use of their condominium on the island of Maui as a place to write and to experience the wonder of God's creation. Much of this book was produced on the lanai of their condo as I looked out at paradise. My staff—Canon SuzeAnne Silla, Sharon Katona, Jon Adamson, Father Henry Randolph, and Angelica Rodela—watched over the diocese with competence and Christian dedication; so competently, in fact, that people hardly knew I was gone. I am blessed to work with marvelous and supportive colleagues! They are companions on the Christian journey and co-workers in the Lord's vineyard.

Nancy Fitzgerald, Rosemi Mederos, Ryan Masteller, and the editorial staff of Morehouse Publishing have assisted me with grace and professionalism during each step of the journey. It is a joy to work with them. They have my thanks and my praise!

Above all, I am deeply and forever grateful to my wife, Sylvia. Without her love and support, my ministry would quickly devolve into self-absorption. She is my reality check, my best friend, my encourager, and my prayer partner.

Joy in the Stocks

Acts 16

I've got that joy, joy, joy, joy
Down in my heart,
Down in my heart,
Down in my heart.
I've got that joy, joy, joy, joy
Down in my heart,
Down in my heart to stay!
And I'm so happy, so very happy,
I've got the love of Jesus in my heart.
Yes, I'm so happy, so very happy,
I've got the love of Jesus in my heart!

The first time I sang that song, it was at some kind of renewal songfest in the late 1970s. I felt like a fraud. I still do.

Don't misunderstand me. The love of Jesus does indeed dwell in my heart. The New Testament promise is clear: "God's love has been poured into our hearts through the Holy Spirit that he has given to us" (Romans 5:5). There is objective truth in that statement, a reminder that we are eternally God's own. "If the Spirit of him who raised Jesus from the dead dwells in you, he who raised Christ from the dead will give life to your mortal bodies also through his Spirit that dwells in you" (Romans 8:11).

And yet when I sing that song (or its many equivalents), I feel . . . well, inauthentic, because I don't generally *feel* anything at all. I know, as a matter of Christian conviction, that I belong to Jesus forever. But why don't I experience the joy that this conviction ought to produce? Most of the time, I can't honestly say, "I'm so happy, so very happy." (Or particularly sad, for that matter!) On the Myers-Briggs Temperament Inventory, I register a strong "T"—a "thinking" type—which means, among other things, that I do not naturally gravitate to the affective side of the scale; I process life through analysis. But a "T" rating doesn't mean that I'm without emotions. I feel sorrow and gladness, love and animosity, fear and anticipation. Yet I can't produce those emotions, or any others, at will—least of all the joy that the song takes for granted. Many Christians, I believe, struggle with that very issue. All around us, our brothers and sisters seem joyful. Why don't we?

St. Paul thinks so highly of joy that he places it second on his list of the "fruit of the Spirit" (see Galatians 5:22–23). When the Holy Spirit begins to transform us from the inside out, gradually reproducing in us the character of Jesus himself, the garden yields a harvest of love, then joy, then peace, then patience, kindness, generosity, faithfulness, gentleness, and self-control. In other words, Paul seems to assume that something is happening inside us. Shouldn't that transformation be part of our experience—a step beyond mere intellectual conviction? If it isn't, what's wrong?

To answer that question, we will take a stroll through St. Paul's Letter to the Christian Church in Philippi. More than any other New Testament document, the Letter to the Philippians glows with joy. St. Paul uses the word "joy" five times in the letter's four chapters, and "rejoice" (which is linguistically related) nine times. Joy permeates the letter from start to finish; sometimes people call it the Epistle of Joy, and rightly so. One Sunday of the Church year—the third Sunday in Advent—is often named Rejoice Sunday because the traditional New Testament reading for that day is taken from Philippians: "Rejoice in the Lord always; again I will say: Rejoice" (4:4). The goal of this book is not so much to understand joy as a concept as it is to see joy in action, as Paul and his Philippian friends dealt with the challenges of following Jesus in the midst of a hostile culture. It was no easier for Paul to be a Christian than it is for us; it was probably, in fact, much harder. Not probably, in fact, but definitely: St. Paul, after all, wrote the Letter to the Philippians from a jail cell.

"I want you to know, beloved, that what has happened to me has actually helped to spread the gospel, so that it has become known throughout the whole imperial guard and to everyone else that my imprisonment is for Christ" (1:12–13). No one knows with certainty where that jail cell was located. Perhaps this was the imprisonment in Rome that concludes the book of Acts, an imprisonment that ended in the apostle's martyrdom during the persecution under the emperor Nero. The final words of the letter (4:21–23) seem to imply a Roman imprisonment. Some scholars, however, propose that the letter was composed from a jail cell in Ephesus. Others suggest Caesarea. Paul mentions "imprisonments" in passing in 2 Corinthians 11:23, which suggests that jail time was a frequent hazard of apostolic life. We will never know with utter assurance where he composed his letter to Philippi.

Wherever the location of the cell, it's clear that Paul's life was in danger. "For to me," Paul says, "living is Christ and dying is gain. If I am to live in the flesh, that means fruitful labor for me; and I do not know which I prefer. I am hard pressed between the two: my desire is to depart and be with Christ, for that is far better; but to remain in the flesh is more necessary for you" (1:21–24). St. Paul is facing his imprisonment—and the possibility of his death—with a calm that, even at two thousand years' distance, we can admire. But the point remains, one potential outcome of this imprisonment was death, and Paul knew it. With the sword dangling over his head, he wrote the Epistle of Joy.

All of this is wonderfully consistent with Paul's personal experience in Philippi, reported in Acts 16. His first visit to the city came at the midpoint of his second missionary journey. Paul and his traveling companions—they included Silas and Timothy, and probably others—had been moving from town to town in central Asia, what we would call Turkey. Initially, the missionaries struggled with their itinerary. "They went through the region of Phrygia and Galatia, having been forbidden by the Holy Spirit to speak the word in Asia" (Acts 16:6). We don't know how the Spirit provided direction. Was it a hunch, an intuitive insight? Or some obstacle that the travelers couldn't overcome? That isn't clear. But in any case, the Spirit's guidance appeared unmistakable. "When they had come opposite Mysia, they attempted to go into Bithynia, but the Spirit of Jesus did not allow them; so, passing by Mysia, they went down to Troas" (Acts 16:7–8). So far, the only thing the Spirit had revealed was where they *shouldn't* go.

But then came a revelation that would change the course of history. "During the night Paul had a vision: there stood a man of Macedonia pleading with him and saying, 'Come over to Macedonia and help us.' When he had seen the vision, we immediately tried to cross over to Macedonia, being convinced that God had called us to proclaim the good news to them" (Acts 16:9–10). Again, we can't, at this distance, know the precise nature of Paul's vision; and in the end, the details aren't important. What matters is that for the first time, the gospel was to be preached on European soil. When Jesus closed a door in Asia, he opened one on a new continent.

Paul and his companions sailed from Troas on the northwest coast of Asia to the city of Samothrace in Macedonia, and from there they passed through Neapolis and arrived at the Roman colony of Philippi, a city with roots going back to the time of Philip, father of Alexander the Great (Acts 16:11–12). (Roman colonies were cities designated by the empire to provide for the needs of army veterans. There, ex-soldiers could settle down, acquire land, and enjoy their retirement with rights equal to the rights of those who lived in Italy.)

Immediately, Paul went to work. "On the sabbath day we went outside by the gate of the river, where we supposed there was a place of prayer; and we sat down and spoke to the women who had gathered there" (Acts 16:13). The "place of prayer" was probably a synagogue, where Jews met to listen to the scriptures and pray. While the heart of Jewish worship was found in the Temple in Jerusalem, over the centuries synagogues had developed as a way for Jews who lived at a distance from their spiritual capital to gather and pray together. Not uncommonly, non-Jews would join them, attracted to the worship of the One God (in contrast to a pantheon of gods) who made high ethical demands of his people. On that Sabbath morning, Paul met one of these "God-fearers" (as Gentile seekers were often known). "A certain woman named Lydia, a worshipper of God, was listening to us; she was from the city of Thyatira and a dealer in purple cloth. The Lord opened her heart to listen eagerly to what was said by Paul. When she and her household were baptized, she urged us, saying, 'If you have judged me to be faithful to the Lord, come and stay in my home.' And she prevailed upon us" (Acts 16:14–15). Lydia was the first European convert to the Christian faith. The riverside encounter in Philippi changed the course of history.

Paul and his friends stayed in Philippi for some time—long enough to get in trouble. As Paul made his way to the place of prayer, he would be followed by a slave-girl with a "spirit of divination." This young woman was in the grip of spiritual evil, an evil that caused her to say the right things for the wrong reason. "These men are servants of the Most High God," she would utter, over and over, "who proclaim to you a way of salvation." The words were true, but something about the tone grated on Paul's nerves. Finally, "very much annoyed, [he] turned and said to the spirit, 'I order you in the name of Jesus Christ to come out of her'" (Acts 16:16–18). Out it came!

The slave-girl's owners, furious that they could no longer use the young woman as a kind of money-making soothsayer, dragged Paul and Silas into court, where they charged them with advocating un-Roman customs. Roman society was as litigious as ours, though the methodology tended to be more extreme! A crowd had gathered and joined in the attack, and the magistrates were won over. They gave orders for Paul and Silas to be flogged, and then they "ordered the jailer to keep them securely. Following these instructions, he put them in the innermost cell and fastened their feet in the stocks" (Acts 16:19–24).

In our culture, we at least attempt to make prisons humane. That was certainly not the case in the ancient world. The Roman government felt no obligation to provide for prisoners' needs. Jails were dark, damp, and crowded. If a prisoner was to eat, family or friends brought the food. Paul and Silas, like many other prisoners, had their feet fastened in the stocks—a device that immobilized the prisoner and forced his legs apart, a dreadfully uncomfortable and humiliating posture. It's precisely at this point in the story that Paul and Silas do the unthinkable. Instead of hatching an escape plan or plotting to take vengeance on the girl's owners or consulting an attorney and trying to find a legal way out of jail, they took a very different approach. "About midnight Paul and Silas were praying and singing hymns to God, and the prisoners were listening to them" (Acts 16:25).

We don't, of course, know what they prayed. The text doesn't tell us. But we can speculate. In the first century, and in our own, Jews pray the psalms, a book that is often called the prayer book of the Bible. Jesus himself prayed psalms on the cross. "My God, my God, why have you forsaken me" (Matthew 27:46; see Psalm 22:1). "Father, into your hands I commend my spirit" (Luke 23:46; see Psalm 31:5). The psalms had so planted themselves in our Lord that, in the moment of intense darkness, they naturally emerged from his heart. And so Paul himself may have prayed the psalms in the darkness of that prison cell. Perhaps it was Psalm 55:6—"O that I had wings like a dove! I would fly away and be at rest." Or Psalm 70:1—"Be pleased, O God to deliver me. O Lord, make haste to help me!" It may be that he combined a plea ("Contend, O Lord, with those who contend with me; fight against those who fight against me" [Psalm 35:1]) with an expression of trust ("Do not fret because of the wicked; do not be envious of wrongdoers . . . Take delight in the Lord, and he will give you the desires of your heart" [Psalm 37:1, 4]). Whatever was the content of Paul and Silas' prayers, light invaded the darkness of the prison cell as they opened their hearts to God.

As it happens, I'm writing these words in the library of a Benedictine monastery—St. Gregory's Abbey in Three Rivers, Michigan. The monks gather seven times a day to pray (at 4:00 a.m., 6:00 a.m., 8:15 a.m., 11:30 a.m., 2:00 p.m., 5:00 p.m., and 7:45 p.m.). The Psalter forms the heart of monastic prayer. Over the course of a week, the monks sing or say all 150 psalms. I can imagine, after doing this for years, that the psalms get into their "bones" (so to speak) and become part of the very fiber of their prayer lives. That may well have been the experience, too, of Paul and of his colleagues, most of whom were Jews steeped in the rhythm of the psalms.

Just as we don't know the content of Paul and Silas' prayers, we are similarly uninformed about the hymns they sang. The New Testament makes it clear that the first Christians were as musical as we. St. Paul encourages his friends in Ephesus to sing "psalms and hymns and spiritual songs, singing and making melody to the Lord in your hearts" (Ephesians 5:19). St. Paul's letters contain what appear to be fragments of early Christian hymns—from the hymn in honor of the humiliated and exalted Christ in Philippians 2:5–11, to a short burst of praise in Ephesians 5:14: "Sleeper, awake! Rise from the dead, and Christ will shine on you." The book of Revelation, from start to finish, is filled with the praise that angels and saints will sing forever in heaven. "Holy, holy, holy, the Lord God, the Almighty, who was and is and is to come" (Revelation 4:8). "Worthy is the Lamb that was slaughtered to receive power and wealth and wisdom and might and honor and glory and blessing!" (Revelation 5:12). "Great and amazing are your deeds, Lord God the Almighty! Just and true are your ways, King of the nations!" (Revelation 15:3). "Hallelujah! For the Lord our God, the Almighty reigns. Let us rejoice and exult and give him the glory" (Revelation 19:6–7a). The business of heaven is worship and praise; this is our eternal destiny, and some day we will join the celestial choir as we worship the living God forever. In that damp, crowded prison cell—surrounded by the noise and smell of their fellow inmates—Paul and Silas imported heaven to earth.

Years before he wrote the Letter to the Philippians, St. Paul encountered joy in a Philippian jail. Immobilized in the stocks, he rejoiced in the Lord. With no release in sight, Paul and Silas prayed and sang hymns. The letter that Paul wrote years later seems strangely consistent with his experience when he first visited Philippi.

It seems right to complete the story of Paul's time in Philippi. God interrupted the hymn singing with an earthquake. Chains fell off the prisoners' limbs, prison doors popped open, and the jailer rushed in, sword in hand, planning to kill himself rather than face the wrath of the magistrates. "Do not harm yourself, for we are all here," Paul says. The jailer, overwhelmed by the fact that the prisoners had not taken advantage of the earthquake's damage, asks Paul and Silas, "Sirs, what must I do to be saved?" Whether this was a spiritual question or merely a practical one isn't important. Paul's answer touched his heart: "Believe on the Lord Jesus, and you will be saved, you and your household." Paul and Silas preach the gospel to the jailer and his family, who, in turn, are baptized. "He and his entire household rejoiced that he had become a believer in God." The next morning, when the magistrates ordered Paul and Silas' release, Paul registers a complaint about the apostles' treatment. "They have beaten us in public, uncondemned," he says, "men who are Roman citizens, and have thrown us into prison; and now are they going to discharge us in secret?" The magistrates realize that they have committed a legal faux pas in ordering Paul's flogging—Paul, after all, was a Roman citizen and thus exempt from such treatment—and they come to the apostles and make an apology (asking them, incidentally, to leave town!). After a final meeting in Lydia's home, Paul and Silas depart for their next adventure in the city of Thessalonica (Acts 16:26–40).

We don't know the particulars of Paul's ongoing relationship with his friends in Philippi. During his third missionary journey, he seems to have passed through Philippi twice, on the way to and from Achaia (which is sometimes simply called "Greece"; see Acts 19:21–22; 20:1–6). Paul's connection with his first European converts remained unusually close, however, and it was this very closeness that provided the occasion for the letter to the Philippians. We will examine this in detail in the last chapter of this book. It will be sufficient to say here that the Christians in Philippi got wind of Paul's arrest (wherever that may have been!) and sent one of their members—a man named Epaphroditus—with a gift of money. (Paul talks about this in Philippians 2:25–30 and 4:10–20.) Epaphroditus became seriously, even desperately, ill during his visit with Paul; and Paul, distressed that his Philippian friends were concerned about Epaphroditus' health, sent him home with a thank-you note, an expression of gratitude for the money and for the friendship that underlies the gift. That note has become the New Testament document that we call the Letter to the Philippians.

Now, a word about what this book isn't as well as what it is. First of all, I won't attempt a thorough exegesis of the text. While much of the letter will make its way into these pages, my analysis will be neither exhaustive nor painstakingly deep. To be sure, I will sometimes refer to the Greek text of Philippians. Our English translations can only go so far in helping us to grasp what Paul is trying to say to his friends—and to us. A single Greek word may point to a whole cluster of meanings that any single English word isn't able to contain. And so, at least occasionally, it will be necessary to unpack a Greek word whose richness cannot be fully conveyed in English.

Nor is this book simply an exercise in meditation. There is certainly a place in Christian devotion for devout and prayerful reading in which a word or a phrase from scripture triggers something in our hearts and takes us rather far afield from the author's original intention. The Spirit is infinitely capable of using scripture in surprising ways, catching us off guard, penetrating our hardened hearts when we least expect it. That may indeed happen here, and some of these reflections will have a meditative quality. But while I will sometimes wander, I will try to keep to a path clearly marked by the text. The letter itself provides the boundaries of our explorations.

Nor is the book intended to be a personal memoir. At times, I will tell stories—about myself, about others—but my biographer would be hard-pressed to construct a coherent history out of these disconnected and generally nonchronological tales. (I should note that sometimes I will change names and details, since many of the stories arise from pastoral situations. It's essential that the privacy of my parishioners, former and current, be honored.) These stories make a simple point that Jesus' story and Paul's and our own do, indeed, interpenetrate. When our stories connect, the coin drops (so to speak), and the gospel takes root in us. That's why I use them.

So what *is* the purpose of this book? Simply this: to answer a question. How can Paul rejoice when he's got nothing (humanly speaking) to rejoice about? How can he talk about joy, joy, joy when he looks down at his feet and sees them encased in stocks? We will listen to him as he writes to his friends in Philippi, and attempt to understand the experience of joy that was both more and less than mere emotion. In a general sort of way, Paul highlights four reasons why joy fills his heart: because of the partnership in the gospel that he shares with his friends in Philippi, because of the unity that they experience in Christ, because of the confidence that they have in Jesus, and because God has poured out upon them his peace, which surpasses understanding. These themes correspond roughly (but not exactly) with the four chapters of the letter and will form the organizing principle of this book.

C. S. Lewis, in his autobiography *Surprised by Joy*, describes joy as a kind of longing that may be triggered by nature or music or literature—but the thing, once we try to grasp, define, and reproduce it, eludes us. When you seek joy as an end in itself, you never find it. Finally, after his conversion, Lewis discovered that Joy itself (he capitalized the word) is only a signpost on the road:

> But what, in conclusion, of Joy? For that, after all, is what the story has mainly been about. To tell you the truth, the subject has lost nearly all interest for me since I became a Christian. I cannot, indeed, complain, like Wordsworth, that the visionary gleam has passed away. I believe (if the thing were at all worth recording) that the old stab, the old bittersweet, has come to me as often and as sharply since my conversion as at any time of my life whatever. But I now know that the experience, considered as a state of my own mind, had never had the kind of importance I once gave it. It was valuable only as a pointer to something other and outer. While that other was in doubt, the pointer naturally loomed large in my thoughts. When we are lost in the woods the sight of a signpost is a great matter. He who first sees it cries, "Look!" The whole party gathers round and stares. But when we have found the road and are passing signposts every few miles, we shall not stop and stare. They will encourage us and we shall be grateful to the authority that set them up. But we shall not stop and stare, or not much; not on this road, though their pillars are of silver and their lettering of gold. "We would be at Jerusalem."[1]

Perhaps we too will discover that joy in the end is only a signpost—a pointer to Jesus himself. Yet it is a signpost that permeates Paul's letter to his friends at Philippi and somehow enabled him to bear witness to Christ in a place of profound darkness. And so, with Paul, we will walk along the road, glancing at the signposts, and remembering that the signposts lead us to our Lord.

It is, admittedly, a journey with some risks. Lewis states, "No doctrine is, for the moment, dimmer to the eye of faith than that which a

---

1. C. S. Lewis, *Surprised by Joy* (New York: Harcourt, Brace and Company, 1956), 238.

man has just successfully defended."[2] Joy, of course is no doctrine; it's a fruit of the Spirit and a marker on the way into the heart of Jesus. But there is a spiritual danger in focusing too much attention upon it. Joy is not, we must remember, an end in itself. As we ponder St Paul's encounter with joy, let us, with him, "regard everything as loss"—*everything,* even joy—"because of the surpassing value of knowing Christ Jesus my Lord" (Philippians 3:8).

---

2. C. S. Lewis, *God in the Dock* (Grand Rapids: William B. Eerdmans, 1970), 128.

PART I

Partnership in the Gospel

"*I* thank my God," St. Paul says, "every time I remember you, constantly praying with joy in every one of my prayers for all of you, because of your sharing in the gospel from the first day until now" (Philippians 1:3–5). The word "sharing" is tricky. It translates the Greek term *kononia*, which the New Testament uses to describe our union with Jesus in the Eucharist (1 Corinthians 10:16), the relationship between Christians in the earliest community of believers (Acts 2:42), our deepest experience of the Holy Spirit (2 Corinthians 13:14), generous and sacrificial care for others in the body of Christ (Hebrews 13:16), and the way that Christians identify and share the sufferings of Jesus himself (Philippians 3:10).

It's almost impossible to translate *kononia* into English without distorting it. Sometimes translators render it as "fellowship," "communion," "sharing," or "partnership," and none of these is fully satisfactory. While the New Revised Standard Version of the Bible translates *kononia* as "sharing" in Philippians 1:5, the New International Version settles on "partnership."

However it's translated, Paul is pointing to a profound truth of the Christian life. We can't do it alone. God designed us to follow Jesus in company with others; and when we do so, the community we form is far more than a gathering of like-minded believers. Our interconnectedness isn't simply a shared theology (though Christians agree on certain basics of belief), nor is it the conviviality of an after-church coffee hour (though Christians, rightly, enjoy spending time together). Our partnership in the gospel binds us together indissolubly, and our bond is eternal. In the first chapter of the Letter to the Philippians, St. Paul identifies at least three elements in this partnership: shared affection, shared proclamation, and shared suffering. We'll look at each in turn and, in the process, see how Jesus binds us both to himself and to one another.

CHAPTER I

Shared Affection

Philippians 1:6–11

I must begin with a confession: I often repeat myself in sermons. Sometimes the repetition is unintentional (a priest once took me aside at the end of a parish visitation and said, "Ed, do you realize that this is the third year in a row that you've used that story about Tom and his prayer life?"), and sometimes it's deliberate. When it comes to Philippians 1:6–11, the repetition is fully intentional. I associate this text with pastoral leave-taking.

I served as a parish priest for twenty-nine years before becoming a bishop, and during that time my moves were relatively infrequent. After two short curacies (the Anglican term for assistantship), I spent eleven years as rector of St. Joseph's Church in Buena Park, California, and almost fourteen years as rector of All Saints Church in Bakersfield, California. When I left Buena Park for Bakersfield in 1986, I found myself drawn to the Philippians passage highlighted in this chapter as I prepared to preach my final sermon. Then, fourteen years later, I returned inexorably (or so it felt) to that same text as I got ready to say goodbye to my friends in Bakersfield. Why? Because in this passage Paul is talking about the deep bonds of affection that have grown between himself and his friends in Philippi. He is saying goodbye to brothers and sisters whose lives have been intertwined with his own. His words could well have been mine.

"It is right for me to think this way about all of you," Paul says, "because you hold me in your heart. . . . For God is my witness, how I long for you with the compassion of Christ Jesus" (1:7a, 8). Paul is speaking with high emotion, and he's talking about a relationship that is far beyond the merely professional. The giveaway is found in the word "compassion," which translates a form of *splanchna*—a Greek term that means, quite literally, "bowels." Yes, bowels. While the word is used in its physical sense only once in the New Testament (take a look at Acts 1:18!), it turns up repeatedly to indicate our deepest emotions. "There is no restriction in our affections," Paul tells the Corinthian Christians (1 Corinthians 6:12). "Refresh my heart in Christ" (Philemon 20), Paul writes his friend Philemon, urging him to forgive his runaway slave Onesimus. Jesus himself displayed the same quality: "When he saw the crowds, he had compassion for them, because they were harassed and helpless, like sheep without a shepherd" (Matthew 9:36). "Affections," "heart," and "compassion" all translate that same, almost unpronounceable, Greek term. When Paul describes his yearning for his friends in Philippi, his heart is fully engaged. That's how it should be in the body of Christ.

In recent years, the Christian church has—quite rightly—recognized the dangers inherent in the relationship between leaders and people. Those relationships include, by definition, an imbalance of power. Pastors are, to put it bluntly, "over" their people; they carry an authority that is both moral and administrative. That's inevitable, whether a church structure is hierarchical or more egalitarian. In our day we have been horrified to see dreadful examples of clergy or lay leaders using that power to take advantage of parishioners—sometimes sexually, sometimes financially, and sometimes more generally in the exercise of authority. People's lives have been destroyed, God's children irreparably damaged, and the church held up to ridicule. And so—again, quite rightly—many churches caution leaders to create appropriate boundary markers, for their own protection and that of their people. In the middle of my office door, for example, is a window, and its purpose is more than purely decorative. My intentions aren't nefarious, but the window signals a kind of transparency in pastoral practice. One can never be too cautious in these matters. The Christian community needs to be assured that its leaders will act in a way that is both professional and ethical.

And yet that very principle of boundary setting, an essential aspect of Christian ministry today, makes it difficult to build the kind of shared affection that cemented the relationship between Paul and his friends at Philippi. How did Paul himself overcome that pastoral conundrum? He identifies two elements.

The first is simultaneously subtle and powerful. It involves *time*. "I am confident of this, that the one who began a good work among you will bring it to completion by the day of Jesus Christ" (1:6). Paul takes the long view. He recognizes that what the Lord is doing in the hearts and minds of the Philippian Christians will unfold, not in weeks and months, but in years and decades, indeed in eternity. "[God] may not come when you want him, but he's always on time," says an old Gospel song; God's timing is not necessarily ours, but it is sure and perfect. Paul comforts himself that, even though he may never see his Philippians friends again in this life, he and they are at a midpoint in their spiritual development. The work of transformation began when Paul first visited Philippi, as Luke describes in Acts 16. The work will not end until they together see Jesus face-to-face in an everlasting reunion. This is the "already/not yet" of the Christian life. (More about this in Chapter 9.) "Beloved, we are God's children now; what we will be has not yet been revealed. What we do know is this: when he is revealed, we will be like him, for we will see him as he is" (1 John 3:2).

It was, I think, sometime in 1973 or 1974 that I was summoned to Esther's hospital bedside. She was one of the elder saints of the parish I served as curate, well into her nineties, beloved and respected, and her family called to say that she was dying. There was no particular illness involved. Her body had simply decided that it was time to shut down. The rector (who'd known Esther for decades) was away on vacation, and the family asked me to visit Esther in his place. And so I made my way to the hospital—to pray and to offer whatever hope and consolation I could.

Esther was wide-awake when I came into the room, weak but still characteristically chatty. She told me that she was prepared to die ("ready to go," were the words she used), that she wasn't afraid, that she looked forward to seeing her long-departed husband, her parents, childhood friends, and, above all, Jesus. Even at a distance of more than thirty years, I can still hear her voice and see her serene face. I stood by her side, took her hand, and prayed, some combination (I recall) of Prayer Bookesque formal language and more spontaneous utterance. Whatever came out, I was aware as I held her hand that she was drifting off to sleep. By the end of the prayer, she was breathing slowly, evenly, and shallowly. I gently released her hand and reached into my wallet for my business card. Then, in the stillness of the room, I wrote her family a note on the back of the card, letting them know that I'd been there and prayed with Esther.

I'm not sure how long I stood next to Esther. Five minutes? Ten? More? She seemed deeply asleep. Then, her eyes still closed, she began to pray—aloud. "God bless Father Ed," she said. "Help him, bless his ministry, keep him in your care." And with that, her voice trailed off and she resumed her even breathing. I will never know (until she and I talk it over in heaven) whether she was aware that I was still in the room. She died that night, her last act to pray for a very young and rather brash priest. Ever since, Revelation's picture has seemed more real to me. In heaven, we're told, incense rises before the Lord as the "prayers of the saints" (Revelation 5:8). Esther's prayers are among them. The Lord had bound us together, created the shared affection that St. Paul describes so vividly in Philippians, and I know, to the very core of my being, that our connection in Christ stretches from time into eternity. Paul had that same confidence as he wrote his friends in Philippi. Affection begins in time and lasts forever, as Jesus transforms us from the inside out.

Paul highlights a second element, *mutual prayer*. "And this is my prayer," he says, "that your love may overflow more and more with knowledge and full insight, to help you to determine what is best, so that in the day of Christ you may be pure and blameless, having produced the harvest of righteousness that comes through Jesus Christ for the glory and praise of God" (1:9–11). Quite commonly (though not without exception), Paul begins his letters by praying for the recipients. In the case of the letter to his Philippian friends, the prayer includes horizontal and vertical ingredients. He prays, to begin with, for an abundance of love among the Philippian Christians (the Greek word is *agape*, the same term used in 1 Corinthians 13 to describe the self-sacrificial love that should characterize the Christian community). As we'll see later in the letter, the Philippians were as "relationally challenged" as any church, their disputes both theological (3:2–3) and personal (4:2–3). It would take a supernatural infusion of God's power to enable them to love one another, and that's precisely what Paul prays for.

His prayer is vertical as well. Paul asks God to produce in the Philippians the discernment to know right from wrong and the holiness of life that will enable them to do it. In other words, transformation doesn't just happen. In praying for his Philippian friends, Paul implies that they will remain untouched by grace unless they consciously open themselves to the Spirit's work.

One of the great gifts that's come to me as Bishop of Northern Indiana is the opportunity to get to know Father Ted Hesburgh, retired president of the University of Notre Dame. Because of Father Ted's friendship with my two predecessor bishops, I've had the chance to sit down with one of the great Christians of our era—a man who loves the Lord Jesus, who reaches out to Christians of all stripes, who is at once intensely loyal to his own church and fully open to people in other Christian communities, who has advised presidents and popes, who has made a significant impact on the relationship between faith and public policy, and who is a force for the Gospel of Jesus Christ around the world and within the church. (Obviously, I find it hard to limit my superlatives when it comes to Father Ted Hesburgh!) On the basis of his warm welcome to me when I first moved to South Bend and the decades-long connection between the diocese and the university, I invited Father Ted to address our diocesan convention in 2002 (and to be designated, in the process, as an honorary canon of our cathedral). Father Ted accepted my invitation, with the caveat that he would need to speak from the heart rather than from a text: his failing eyesight no longer allows him the luxury of writing out his speeches. I happily agreed. What struck me most from Father Ted's remarks was a single piece of advice, one that I carry in my heart daily. Every day, Father Ted said, Christians should pray a simple prayer: "Come, Holy Spirit." In that prayer, we are allowing God to fill in the gaps and to accomplish in us what he wants to accomplish.

And so it is that Paul the Apostle prays for his friends in Philippi. His prayer is at once specific and open-ended. He is asking God to do what needs to be done to transform the lives of these Christian converts; and having prayed, he places them in the Lord's most ample care. In other words, Paul's short and direct prayer provides a kind of spiritual "glue" that binds him to his friends in Philippi and permits him, even from the distance of a jail cell, to express the affection that wells up in his heart. "Come, Holy Spirit," he says in effect, "touch my friends and transform them. Come, Holy Spirit, help them to know your purpose and to do it." Paul maintains just the right balance in his role with the Philippian Christians as their leader and friend. He recognizes two things: that their relationship expresses itself over time, with the present moment as a kind of way station on the journey; and that the relationship is nurtured and sustained, above all, by prayer that gives God permission (not that he needs it!) to work in their lives. The *Book of Common Prayer* captures this well: "Almighty God, we entrust those who are dear to us to thy never-failing care and love, for this life and the life to come, knowing that thou art doing for them better things than we can desire or pray for; through Jesus Christ our Lord. *Amen.*"[1]

The shared affection that Paul portrays in the opening sentences of Philippians isn't exclusively a matter of feelings. There's an objective reality that underlies his words. Jesus has bound us to one another—in 1 Corinthians 12:12–13, Paul identifies this as a baptismal reality—as surely as he has bound us to himself. Nothing can change that. Thus, the church is more like a family than an organization. Our family connections are a given. You cannot choose *not* to be the child of your parents, the sibling of your siblings, the niece or nephew of your uncle. You are related to them whether you like it or not. So it is in the body of Christ. As brothers and sisters of Jesus and children of the Father, we are by definition related to one another. When we refer to a fellow Christian as a brother or sister, the term is not simply an analogy. It's a statement of fact.

---

1. *Book of Common Prayer* (New York: Oxford University Press, 1979), 831.

And yet, within the family, affection grows—not easily, to be sure—in fits and starts, sometimes (because the church has its share of challenging people, it's important to be honest about this) not at all. But we can profitably reflect on the people whose faithfulness has challenged our own, brothers and sisters who have encouraged us in our own journeys, shown us Jesus in surprising ways, provoking us (as the Letter to the Hebrews so colorfully puts it in 10:24) to love and good deeds. Out of the apparent randomness of our connection in the body of Christ, God creates shared affection.

A couple of years ago, during a vacation trip to Southern California, I found myself driving almost accidentally by St. Joseph's Church in Buena Park, in the northwest corner of Orange County, and decided to stop and walk around the deserted buildings. I'd left St. Joseph's two decades earlier, and in the intervening years, the parish had installed an outdoor columbarium on the south side of the parish hall building. Though I had occasionally visited the parish since my departure, this was the first time I was able to stand before the columbarium and contemplate the name plates that line the wall. There, in one corner, was Bill, my former senior warden and a great counselor to me in my early (and brash) years in the parish. (Bill's son is now a bishop. How proud he'd be!) Toward the center I saw Ellen's name. She was once my altar guild directress, unfailingly cheerful, amazingly flexible, always ready to say yes whenever I tinkered with the liturgy. In another corner was Jerry, a gifted evangelist. Whenever newcomers would visit the church on Sunday morning, Jerry would identify them (he had a kind of internal radar that would help him to spot new people) and shepherd them around the coffee hour, introducing the newcomers to as many parishioners as possible. Then there was Sarah, president of the Episcopal Church Women, as direct and honest a person as I've ever known, with a tough exterior and a heart softened to the Lord—and to those in pain. She was a born pastor. The list went on and on as I looked up and down the rows of the columbarium. It took me quite by surprise (because I don't easily show emotions) when I found myself weeping in gratitude for these brothers and sisters.

As we ponder the people to whom we are bound in Christ, names and faces will appear before us, some living, many dead. These are the ones who have shaped us and formed us in the Christian life. "Since we are surrounded by so great a cloud of witnesses, let us also lay aside every weight and the sin that clings so closely, and let us run with perseverance the race that is set before us, looking to Jesus the pioneer and perfecter of our faith" (Hebrews 12:1–2). The shared affection that grows almost unbidden in the body of Christ has the power to transform us, to challenge us, and to provide a model for faithful discipleship. In this, St. Paul discovered his joy, and so do we.

Questions for Reflection

1. Who are the people, living or dead, to whom you are bound?

2. Who are the ones who have borne witness to you and shaped your life as a Christian?

3. Who first introduced you to Jesus or made the gospel real to you? How did that happen? Was it verbal witness, personal example, or some combination?

4. Who continues to do so now?

CHAPTER 2

Shared Proclamation

Philippians 1:12–18

I can still remember with surprising clarity the first Christian sermon I ever heard. In the spring of 1966, my girlfriend (later fiancée, now wife) invited me to Hollywood First Presbyterian Church to hear Dr. Raymond Lindquist. I was a recent convert to the Christian faith and as unchurched (to use the modern term) as one could be. The sermon that day changed my life forever.

On one level, Dr. Lindquist's sermon was hardly groundbreaking. He took 2 Timothy 4:6–15 as his text. The apostle is apparently just months from martyrdom, and he writes to his young apprentice and successor, Timothy, with some final words of advice. At first, Paul reflects on his impending death. "As for me, I am already being poured out as a libation, and the time of my departure has come" (2 Timothy 4:6). He looks back at his ministry and the way that he has faithfully done the Lord's bidding. "I have fought the good fight, I have finished the race, I have kept the faith. From now on there is reserved for me the crown of righteousness, which the Lord, the righteous judge, will give me on that day, and not only to me but also to all who have longed for his appearing" (2 Timothy 4:7–8). Paul seems to be at peace with himself and with God, despite the sword that hangs over him.

But then, in a moment of painful honesty, Paul tells Timothy about the people who've let him down. "Do your best to come to me soon, for Demas, in love with this present world, has deserted me and gone to Thessalonica; Crescens has gone to Galatia, Titus to Dalmatia. . . . Alexander the coppersmith did me great harm; the Lord will repay him for his deeds" (2 Timothy 4:9–10, 14). Although Paul mentions those who remain loyal to him (2 Timothy 4:11–13), it is obvious that he feels alone, abandoned. That, in fact, was the title of Dr. Lindquist's sermon: "When You Feel Abandoned." He spent some time talking about ways in which we, like Paul, can experience abandonment, and about Paul's only antidote (trusting, despite his current circumstances, that God had used his ministry and that his eternal future is secure). We too, said Dr. Lindquist, need in moments of desolation to recognize in faith both the presence of the Lord in our lives and the promise of everlasting life that is both sure and certain. End of sermon.

Two things happened to me that day. First, I had an "aha!" moment. The scriptures became real to me in a way that they hadn't before. I felt as though Paul wrote his letter to *me*, that these ancient words had been penned not only for Timothy's benefit but also for mine. Second, I found myself saying, "I want to do that, too." In an instant, Jesus laid out my life's work: "to make the word of God fully known" (Colossians 1:25); to take a two thousand-year-old text and proclaim it today so that lives (including my own) might be transformed by its power.

That very power is the experience to which St. Paul bears witness as he writes to his friends in Philippi. He has discovered that the word of God has the power to transform lives and to affect the eternal destinies of men and women. He is convinced that the proclamation that he and the Philippians share is God's vehicle for changing the world.

The context is bittersweet. "I want you to know, beloved, that what has happened to me has actually helped to spread the gospel, so that it has become known throughout the whole imperial guard and to everyone else that my imprisonment is for Christ" (1:12–13). So far, so good. Paul's incarceration is enough of a public event that it has gained the attention of people well beyond the Christian community. His very body, held fast in the stocks, has become an icon of the gospel, a visible sign of Jesus himself. Paul's imprisonment has also emboldened

Christians. "Most of the brothers and sisters, having been made confident in the Lord by my imprisonment, dare to speak the word with greater boldness and without fear" (1:14). Perhaps Paul's own fearlessness in the face of horrendous circumstances has provided just the encouragement that his fellow believers need so that they too can proclaim the gospel boldly.

But then Paul points to the dark side of his imprisonment. His leadership role in the church was not, apparently, universally embraced; and so some rivals took advantage of the power vacuum created by his imprisonment to challenge his apostleship and to advance their own cause. "Some proclaim Christ from envy and rivalry, but others from goodwill. These proclaim Christ out of love, knowing that I have been put here for the defense of the gospel; the others proclaim Christ out of selfish ambition, not sincerely but intending to increase my suffering in my imprisonment" (1:15–17). When Paul writes about the power of proclamation, he himself is powerless: not only shackled (that's bad enough), but also marginalized and even despised by his rivals. Yet he never loses confidence in the gospel and the power that's unleashed when it is faithfully proclaimed. It's important to note that Paul's rivals are not proclaiming the kind of alternative gospel that he attacks in Galatians (e.g., Galatians 1:6–9). No, the content of these rivals' preaching is apparently unexceptional. The motives behind the preaching, however, are decidedly murky.

What does Paul mean when he talks about proclamation? A Greek word gives us some hints. In Philippians 1:15–16, what's twice translated as "proclaim" renders the verb *kerusso*, which itself derives from *kerux*, referring to a herald. The job of a herald is to make a public proclamation. If a king decides to tax his people, for example, the herald goes out into the public square and announces the taxation. He doesn't argue for it or make the king's case or describe in detail the nuances of the new tax code. No, the *kerux* simply says, "Here it is." And that, by analogy, is the job of the Christian herald. Preachers announce the good news. They announce it publicly and forcefully, not so much by argument as by declaration. Here it is. Or, more precisely, here *he* is. The role of the Christian *kerux* isn't to create a new message but faithfully to pass on the announcement entrusted to him or her by the King.

The message itself, unadorned, has the power to transform the lives of its hearers. When the pig Wilbur is threatened with death, his friend Charlotte, the spider, weaves into her web over the pigpen the words, SOME PIG. The words trigger a series of events that rescue Wilbur from slaughter and change forever Wilber's place in the world.[1] Nothing complicated is going on here. Charlotte's message is sheer proclamation—with earth-shaking results. And so Paul tells his friends that he and they must tell the story, make it known, and entrust the outcome to the Holy Spirit, who is infinitely capable of infusing our words with supernatural power. We never become so sophisticated that we are beyond the basics of the life, death, and resurrection of Jesus. We can never hear the story too often. Until Jesus comes again and the world as we know it is metamorphosed into the New Jerusalem, the message will continue to bear fruit in transformed lives. Some Lord! "So shall my word be that goes out from my mouth; it shall not return to me empty, but it shall accomplish that which I shall purpose, and succeed in the thing for which I sent it" (Isaiah 55:11).

I'm now addressing my fellow Episcopalians, though I suspect that the following observations will apply well beyond my own Christian community. We tend to be ambivalent about proclamation, about the power of words to penetrate the human heart. As sacramental people, we rejoice in encountering Jesus in the Eucharist—and often, in the process, tend to undervalue the ways that we meet him in the word proclaimed. Once, on vacation far from my own diocese, I visited a church that proudly printed its mission statement on the front page of the Sunday bulletin. It read, "St. Swithin's is a small, friendly parish with short sermons." Period. (I'm not making this up.) What does such a "mission statement" imply? That the sermon is at best an unpleasant necessity that, while required in the rubrics of the *Book of Common Prayer*, should be dispatched as quickly and as painlessly as possible. Indeed, many Episcopalians delight in paraphrasing St. Francis of Assisi, who once said, "Preach the gospel at all times. If necessary, use words." That's true enough (more about that later in this chapter, in fact). We've all heard

---

1. E. B. White, *Charlotte's Web* (New York: Harper & Row, 1952), 77.

preaching that is shallow or strident or milquetoast or rigidly dogmatic or terminally trendy. Such preaching can embitter us and make us wary of the whole enterprise of proclamation. But here is precisely where the danger lies: we can end up so denigrating the spoken word that we deny its urgency and its power.

In his Letter to the Philippians, Paul uses shorthand to describe the work of proclamation. A series of phrases—"spread the gospel," 1:12; "speak the word," 1:14; "proclaim Christ," 1:15–17—identify the task without defining the content. We have to look elsewhere to see what he's referring to. In his First Letter to the Corinthians, Paul responds to a kind of watered-down, desupernaturalized version of the gospel that's gained traction in Corinth. And so he reminds his Corinthian parishioners about the central thrust of the Christian message:

> I handed on to you as of first importance what I in turn had received: that Christ died for our sins in accordance with the scriptures, and that he was buried, and that he was raised on the third day in accordance with the scriptures, and that he appeared to Cephas, then to the twelve. Then he appeared to more than five hundred brothers and sisters at one time, most of whom are still alive, though some have died. Then he appeared to James, then to all the apostles. Last of all, as to one untimely born, he appeared also to me. (1 Corinthians 15:3–8)

Paul's message represents the convergence of two stories. First, there's the story of Jesus himself—and, particularly, his death, resurrection, and subsequent appearances. If we wander from these events, we endanger our ability to proclaim the gospel. They are at the heart of the Christian faith, the irreducible minimum of proclamation. Second, there's Paul's own story, referred to almost by title ("Last of all . . . "). We read these words in light of the fuller account of Paul's conversion in the book of Acts (it appears three times, in Acts 9:1–18; 22:1–21; and 26:2–23, with only minor variations) and Paul's own description in Galatians 1:13–24. Proclamation occurs when the story of Jesus and our own story intersect. "Christ died . . . and last of all . . ." Whatever form our proclamation takes, it must make a connection between the events of two thousand years ago and the events of our own lives. I suspect that's why Dr. Lindquist's sermon in 1966 had such a profound impact on my life. He made a connection between the ancient text and my own struggles, between Paul's sense of abandonment and the times when I've felt abandoned, between the comfort that Paul experienced in the darkness of death row and the comfort that I, as a new Christian, had encountered when I met Jesus Christ.

I mentioned that St. Francis's advice is often imprecisely used, as a way of devaluing the spoken word. Having said that, I should add that St. Francis is actually right. We can, in fact, proclaim the gospel in a myriad of ways: word, deed; sermon, song; acts of compassion, a warm smile, a helping hand, a word of encouragement. Like Paul in his prison cell, we ourselves are icons of Christ, visible signs of the presence of Jesus. Every sentence we speak and every gesture we make can enhance or impede the gospel. Sometimes, indeed, Jesus is proclaimed in surprising, almost breathtaking ways.

So it was, a few years ago, that I was visiting a parish at the southern end of my diocese. (The Sunday work of a bishop generally involves what's called a "visitation," in which the bishop preaches, celebrates the Eucharist, sometimes baptizes and confirms, often meets with the parish leadership. In a small diocese like my own, I'm able to visit each parish about once a year.) During the opening procession, I noticed a young woman in the third or fourth row who was obviously living with some degree of a developmental disability. She appeared to be in her twenties or early thirties, and she sat between two adults—apparently her parents—who held the hymnal for her and pointed at the words on the page. During the first part of the liturgy, I found myself watching this young woman and wondering what the service meant to her. Did the words make sense? Did she understand the scriptures as they were read? What about the sermon? I try to avoid complex concepts and stick to the basics, but was she able to grasp even that? My heart reached out to her, but I was unable to penetrate the mask of her face. But then God answered my question.

The service bulletin indicated that, during the offertory (the time when money is collected and when bread and wine are placed on the altar for the Eucharist), there was to be a solo. To be honest, I'm involved enough in the service at that point that I tend not to hear whatever's

being sung, not by choice but by the flurry of liturgical events. (I suspect that choir directors around my diocese are gasping as they read that
sentence.) But this time, the solo caught my attention. It was the young
woman, who stood up in place, held a song book, and began to sing the
old Gospel song often associated with Billy Graham crusades:

> O Lord my God, when I in awesome wonder
> Consider all the worlds Thy hands have made,
> I see the stars, I hear the rolling thunder.
> Thy power throughout the universe displayed.
> Then sings my soul, my Savior God, to Thee:
> How great Thou art, how great Thou art!
> Then sings my soul, my Savior God, to Thee:
> How great Thou art, how great Thou art![2]

That may be the most powerful proclamation I've ever heard. She sang
with her whole heart, and I knew that she knew how great God is. Her
story and the story of Jesus intersected in her song, a seamless inter-
weaving of gospel truth and a life open to the Spirit's touch. In the crush
of people after the Eucharist, I never had the chance to thank her; and
so I write this as my tribute to a mighty disciple of Jesus.

Paul ends this section with a reflection on joy. "What does it matter?" he asks (referring to the fact that some preach Christ for the best
of reasons and some, sadly, out of bitterness and rivalry). "Just this, that
Christ is proclaimed in every way, whether out of false motives or true;
and in that I rejoice" (1:18). Paul and his friends in Philippi share a common value. They have all experienced the transforming work of the gospel, and they all know what happens when Jesus is faithfully proclaimed.
This isn't mere theory to them. It's a reality that has touched their hearts
as well as their minds. From the first conversation with Lydia to Paul's
encounter with the Philippian jailer, Paul and his friends had seen how
the Spirit can take human words and give them supernatural power.

And what about us? I find myself wondering about the power of
proclamation today. We live in an era when technology changes daily.

---

2. *The Baptist Hymnal* (Carol Stream, IL: Hope Publishers, 1990), Hymn 21.

The spoken word often gives way—to the magic of special effects, to digital imagery, to the miracle of instant global communication through the Internet. We hardly give it a second thought when we click a mouse key and our words appear on a computer screen in Sub-Saharan Africa. Yet the most powerful form of communication remains person-to-person and face-to-face. Nothing can replace the spiritual power that's released when Christians connect their own story with the story of Jesus. And for Paul and for his friends in Philippi, nothing could replace the joy that they knew when Jesus is faithfully proclaimed. Like them, Jesus invites us to "dare to speak the word with greater boldness and without fear" (1:14).

QUESTIONS FOR REFLECTION

1. How has the gospel been most effectively proclaimed to you?

2. What were (and are) the qualities that made it effective? What grabbed your attention and helped you to listen?

3. What made you open to hearing the gospel, receiving its message?

4. How is Jesus challenging you to share in the ministry of proclamation?

CHAPTER 3

Shared Suffering

Philippians 1:7b, 27–30

ARE YOU AFRAID TO DIE?

*I*n the late 1990s, I had the privilege of taking part in a short-term mission trip to the Diocese of South Rwenzori in Uganda. Under the auspices of Sharing of Ministries Abroad, an Anglican mission agency (SOMA), five Americans and one Ugandan traveled to Kasese in the southwestern corner of the country for a week of teaching and prayer with the clergy of the diocese. Kasese is overshadowed by the Rwenzori Mountains, which rise in spectacular folds to fifteen thousand feet, their lower levels encased in lush vegetation, their upper regions barren and alpine. What our team didn't know before we arrived in Kasese was that the mountains were home to a rebel insurgency known as the Allied Democratic Forces (ADF), an Islamic group committed to the overthrow of the legitimate government of Uganda. (The ADF has since been neutralized, though other insurgencies continue to plague the country.) At night, ADF terrorists would creep down from their mountainous hideouts and commit atrocities on the local population. Our team visited refugee camps where local citizens, driven from their homes, found at least a semblance of safety (though the living conditions were grim). War took on a human and tragic face for us.

One evening, as the team sat on the porch of Bishop Zebedee Masereka's home, we read a newspaper from the capital city of Kampala and stumbled across an article about an atrocity in the Kasese area. A group of rebels, the article said, had attacked some travelers as they crossed the Katwe bridge, dragged them into the bush, and mutilated them horribly. (The article described the mutilations in graphic detail.) Someone on the team grabbed a map and discovered that the Katwe bridge was only a few miles from the bishop's home. More than that, our team was scheduled a few days later to visit a parish in a corner of the diocese that would require us to cross that same bridge. As we sat on the bishop's porch and the sun sank behind the Rwenzori Mountains, our voices became more and more shrill. What if the rebels are waiting for us? What if we're dragged out into the bush? What if unspeakable horrors are perpetrated on our bodies?

The team had been joined that evening by a young Church Army officer named Beatrice. (The Church Army is the Anglican equivalent of the Salvation Army, a lay ministry that combines evangelism and social service with great integrity.) Beatrice sat in silence as the Americans catastrophized about the Katwe bridge. Our imaginations (mine, certainly) became increasingly vivid, our voices (mine, certainly) increasingly shrill. Finally, Beatrice broke in. She asked a simple question, and sounded surprised, almost incredulous: "Are you afraid to die?"

This young woman lived with death every day. She wasn't a visitor to Kasese; it was her home. Every time the sun went down, she faced the possibility of being dragged out of her bed by ADF rebels. This was no theory to her; colleagues and friends had suffered precisely that fate. This had forced her, of course, to deal with ultimate issues. What does it mean to suffer? Was she willing to die for her Lord? If Jesus asked her to make that sacrifice, would she do so wholeheartedly? Or would she seek a less painful alternative? Beatrice's question forced all of us to confront our own fears. Almost ten years later, I can still hear her voice and I still ask myself that same question. "Are you afraid to die?" Am I afraid of what Jesus might require of me? Whatever hardships he might send my way, would I seek a less painful alternative? Would I avoid (metaphorically speaking) the Katwe bridge?

For St. Paul, death—not natural death, but death at the hand of others, death for the sake of Jesus—was a daily possibility. It is true that, in Paul's day, the church had not yet experienced systematic persecution. That was for later generations. Instead, persecution tended to be ad hoc and occasional. Religious officials in Jerusalem, of course, had not only conspired with the Roman government to crucify Jesus but they were also actively attacking the new Christian movement. Around the Mediterranean basin, Christianity was a sufficiently new phenomenon on the religious scene that it hadn't attracted full-blown official attention. Certainly, at the core of the gospel was an affirmation that would in later decades put it at odds with the Roman Empire. Pinching incense into a bowl in front of a statue of the emperor and saying, "Caesar is Lord," represented the duty of every citizen. For Christians, "Jesus is Lord" (1 Corinthians 12:3; Philippians 2:11) was the first creed. Thus, the gospel contained seeds that would inevitably bring it into conflict with the empire. "Jesus is Lord" would ultimately be seen as a deeply subversive proclamation, a dangerous denial of the lordship of Caesar. But as Paul traveled around the eastern end of the Mediterranean, his troubles were more localized. He regularly offended synagogue leaders and government officials, and that led to the laundry list of suffering that he provides us in 2 Corinthians 11:23–28 and to the prison cell from which he wrote the Letter to the Philippians.

Paul makes it clear that his Philippian friends are suffering with him, and he with them. "All of you share in God's grace with me, both in my imprisonment and in the defense and confirmation of the gospel" (Philippians 1:7). This is a startling statement. He calls suffering a *grace*. It isn't simply an accident that comes upon us, a series of unfortunate but basically random events. (Think of the children's books by Lemony Snicket and the movie based on them.) No, Paul says, in some way beyond our imagining, Jesus invites us to embrace suffering, to see below its harsh exterior the outworking of God's overwhelming love. Or perhaps, more accurately, Jesus invites us to recognize in the midst of suffering the opportunity to encounter him more profoundly than in any other setting: not so much that Jesus sends the suffering, but rather that the suffering thrusts us into the arms of Jesus and of one another.

There's a hint of this shared experience toward the end of the first chapter. "Only, live your life in a manner worthy of the gospel of Christ," he says, "so that, whether I come and see you or am absent and hear about you, I will know that you are standing firm in one spirit, striving side by side with one mind for the faith of the gospel" (1:27). A couple of items stand out. First, the expression "live your life" translates the Greek verb *politeuo*—which refers to conducting yourself appropriately as a citizen. This would have special meaning for the Christians in Philippi, a Roman colony filled with former soldiers who had been granted the privilege of Roman citizenship. Paul seems to be pointing to a solemn obligation, living in a way that's congruent with our citizenship not just on earth but above all in heaven (see also 3:20). We are subjects, after all, of the King of kings. Second, he reminds his friends in Philippi that their lives are bound together irrevocably. He piles phrase upon phrase to make this point: "one spirit . . . side by side . . . one mind." The suffering that inevitably comes to Christians must be borne together. Paul's vision of the Christian life is light years from a kind of individualized, me-and-Jesus-against-the-world attitude that can sometimes characterize Western expressions of the faith.

The Apostle drives the point home by adding a grim word about his opponents. "This [your joint striving with me] is evidence of their destruction, but of your salvation. And this is God's doing" (1:28). The Lord won't forget your faithfulness in the face of suffering, he tells his friends; you can be assured of your eternal place in the heart of God, nor—this is the painful part—will the Lord forget the faithlessness of those who so actively oppose the gospel that they refuse God's unconditional offer of reconciliation. The difficult truth here is that God won't force *anyone* into a relationship with him. If we wish to say no to him, that is our privilege. Remember the famous nineteenth-century Holman Hunt painting of the Jesus' invitation "Behold, I stand at the door and knock" (Revelation 3:20). Jesus stands at a door that has no outside handle. It can only be opened from within. Jesus won't make a forced entry. In this passage, Paul reminds his friends in Philippi of the terrible consequences of a settled rejection of the gospel.

Having said that, Paul returns to the theme of shared suffering: "For he has graciously granted you the privilege not only of believing in Christ, but of suffering for him as well—since you are having the same struggle that you saw that I had and now hear that I still have" (1:29–30). The word "suffering," incidentally, is a strong one. The Greek verb is *pascho*, root of our word "passion," which Christians frequently use to describe the suffering and death of Jesus. The long Gospel accounts of Jesus' betrayal, arrest, trial, torture, and death are often called Passion narratives. *Pascho* appears in the Gospels—for example, when Jesus predicts his death (see Matthew 16:21; 17:12, among many references)—as well as in Peter's description of Jesus' suffering (1 Peter 2:23). Paul is telling his friends that he and they share in a suffering that was first borne by the Lord Jesus and that now binds them together.

What is our equivalent? Clearly Christians in the West today don't live with the same kind of persecution that Paul and his friends faced. Our faith isn't proscribed. We can practice it in any way we want. Sometimes, of course, Christians sensationalize legal challenges to publicly supported signs of faith and turn those challenges into marks of malignant intent. When the American Civil Liberties Union (ACLU) sues the government for the removal of a cross on public land or a Christian club in a public high school is denied access to a classroom, we often hear cries of persecution. While the culture we live in may be hostile to the faith (or, at least, indifferent; more about that later), nothing prevents us either believing, teaching, or sharing our faith. Whatever parallel we find between Paul's situation and our own, it isn't that the government is trying to wipe us out. (Yes, there are places on the planet where Christians are indeed forbidden to practice their faith and where any expression—public or private—is forbidden. In some parts of the Islamic world, for example, it is dangerous to be a Christian. We live in an era when Christians continue to be martyred for their faith, but that terrible reality is beyond the scope of this book.) The suffering that we experience is more subtle.

Jane Austen's *Mansfield Park* tells the story of the courtship of Edmund Bertram (second son of a gentry family) and his poor relation, Fanny Price. While Mr. Bertram will not inherit his father's estate, he is nonetheless wealthy and a desirable "catch"—so desirable, in fact, that the worldly Mary Crawford has set her sights on him. But then Miss Crawford discovers to her horror that Mr. Bertram intends to become a priest of the Church of England. (I cite this example not because a priestly calling represents a kind of Christian "gold standard," but because it illustrates the fact that Christian faith was as marginalized two hundred years ago as it is now.)

Miss Crawford began with the following statement:

"So you are to be a clergyman, Mr. Bertram. This is rather a surprise to me."

"Why should it surprise you? You must be designed for some profession, and might perceive that I am neither a lawyer, nor a soldier, nor a sailor."

"Very true; but, in short, it had not occurred to me. And you know there is generally an uncle or a grandfather to leave a fortune to the second son."

"A very praiseworthy practice," said Edmund, "but not quite universal. I am one of the exceptions, and being one, must do something for myself."

"But why are you to be a clergyman? I thought that was always the lot of the youngest, where there were so many to choose before him."

"Do you think the church itself never to be chosen, then?"

"Never is a black word. But yes, in the never of conversation which means not very often, I do think it. For what is to be done in the church? Men love to distinguish themselves, and in either of the other lines, distinction may be gained, but not in the church. *A clergyman is nothing* . . . I am just as much surprised now as I was at first that you should intend to take orders. You are really fit for something better. Come, do change your mind. It is not too late. Go into the law."[1]

Lest we romanticize the past, it's important to remember that then—as now—serious Christian expression has always been on the margins of the culture. Then—as now—our values, priorities, and daily decisions may put us at odds with our families, our friends, and our co-workers. We're

---

1. Jane Austen, *Mansfield Park* (1814; New York: Signet Classics, 1996), 95–97 (italics mine).

looking at life through different lenses. Alan Jacobs, in his recent biography of C. S. Lewis, notes that after Lewis's conversion, his household objected strenuously to his new practice of Sunday church attendance. He had never had any particular Sunday duties prior to his conversion; but suddenly, his presence on Sunday morning became utterly indispensable. As Lewis commented in an interview, "It is extraordinary how inconvenient to your family it becomes for you to get up early to go to Church. It doesn't matter so much if you get up early for anything else, but if you get up early to go to Church, it's very selfish of you and you upset the house."[2]

Paul talks about sharing the same struggle (the Greek word is *agona*, root of the English "agony") with his friends in Philippi (1:30). Perhaps the very struggles that we face every day, our daily attempts to apply the Christian faith at work or at home or at school, represent the *agona* of Christian discipleship in the new millennium. The Christian life is cruciform; but the way that we encounter the cross varies from era to era, from culture to culture, and from person to person. It may simply involve our willingness to forsake everything that separates us from God, from his will for our lives, and from the world for which Jesus died. "Do you renounce Satan and all the spiritual forces of wickedness that rebel against God? Do you renounce the evil powers of this world which corrupt and destroy the creatures of God? Do you renounce all sinful desires that draw you from the love of God?"[3] We could spend our entire lives discovering what these questions mean and never exhaust their depth.

We must not, on the other hand, forget that Christians sometimes must put their lives on the line for Jesus' sake—even in our tolerant and pluralistic culture. This leads me to the story of Richard Morrisroe.

A couple of years before the writing of this book, Father Richard Phelps, rector of the Church of the Good Shepherd in East Chicago, Indiana, invited me to spend a day with him. East Chicago may be the poorest city within the borders of the Diocese of Northern Indiana.

---

2. Alan Jacobs, *The Narnian: The Life and Imagination of C. S. Lewis* (New York: HarperSanFrancisco, 2006), 224.

3. *Book of Common Prayer* (New York: Oxford University Press, 1979), 302.

The community is predominantly African American and Hispanic; urban blight and decayed buildings mar the city's landscape; drug use and crime dominate the city's life. In the face of that crushing poverty, Father Richard does heroic work. A constant stream of people comes to his door for help (to the point that it's almost impossible to sit in his living room and have an uninterrupted conversation with him). I am always deeply moved when I see the countless lives touched by this tiny parish and its devoted priest.

When I visited East Chicago that day, Father Richard introduced me to Richard Morrisroe, the city's planning director. Richard had once been a Roman Catholic priest and is now an active and faithful lay member of that church, married and a father and grandfather. As we got to know one another, Richard told me the story of his encounter with Jonathan Daniels.

In the summer of 1965, Dr. Martin Luther King issued a plea for people to come to the South and help him to register African American voters—and Richard joined the southward pilgrims. So did Jonathan Daniels, a student at the Episcopal Theological School in Cambridge, Massachusetts, and thousands of others who committed themselves to full and equal rights for America's black citizens. For some weeks, Richard and Jonathan plunged into the task of voter registration. On August 13, as part of a group of twenty-nine people picketing an all-white store, they were arrested, jailed (in dreadful and unsanitary conditions), and finally released six days later. Following their release, Richard and Jonathan—along with Ruby Sales, a young African American woman— walked up the steps into a small market in Hayneville, Alabama, where they intended to buy sodas. A man appeared at the door, shotgun in hand, threatening Ruby. In a single motion, Jonathan shoved Ruby aside and the shotgun fired a blast, killing Jonathan instantly. A second shot seriously injured Richard Morrisroe. (Jonathan Daniel's martyrdom is commemorated on the Episcopal Church's liturgical calendar on August 14.) Richard spent months recovering from his injuries, and (he told me) the experience changed him forever. Thirty-two years after the events of August 13, in the summer of 1997, Richard returned to Haynesville for a commemoration of Jonathan Daniels' martyrdom, and he reflected on what had brought him and his companions south.

"We were young when we were here," he said. "We were too young to respect the boundaries between black and white, and South and North, and those who had money and those who didn't."[4] To this day, Richard has dedicated his life to the cause of justice. His work among the poorest of the poor in East Chicago is the direct result of the suffering that he shared with Jonathan and with African Americans in the segregated South. It transformed him; and hearing his story, Jesus touched me as well and opened an unexpected vista into his joy.

When Paul ponders his own suffering, he is able to affirm it as a grace (1:7), in large part because he doesn't suffer alone. He suffers in company with a community of disciples. "My brothers and sisters," says James, brother of our Lord, "whenever you face trials of any kind, consider it nothing but joy" (James 1:2). St. Paul would agree with this counterintuitive insight, because his suffering has bound him more deeply to his friends in Philippi. We follow Jesus together, Paul tells us, and we suffer for Jesus together.

QUESTIONS FOR REFLECTION

1. How is Jesus inviting you to embrace the cruciform life?

2. In what ways have you experienced suffering for the sake of Jesus? Do those sufferings in any way mirror the baptismal renunciations?

3. How has that suffering bound you to your fellow Christians? (Or has it?)

4. As you have responded to the suffering of others, how has that affected your relationship with them?

---

4. *NewsBank*, http://nl.newsbank.com/nl-search/we/Archives?p_action=doc&p_doc id=0EADDCC0E8E29EBE&

PART II

Unity in Christ

*W*hen I was in college, I lived for a year on a street graced by the presence of three churches. The first, next door to my apartment complex, was the True Love Church. Just down the block stood the Greater True Love Church. A bit farther on was the Reformed Greater True Love Church. It didn't take much imagination for me to conjure up the scenarios: church fight, division, another fight, another split, on and on and on. Whatever the issues—were they theological, ethical, personal?—those three churches bore testimony to a sad truth. Schism leads to schism. I can't help wondering how many churches I'd find on that block today, almost four decades later! Perhaps the most difficult word in the Nicene Creed is "one": "We believe in one holy catholic and apostolic Church."[1] *One?* The reality we experience every day belies the affirmation and makes it seem like a comic distortion of the "facts on the ground."

The Christian church is hardly a hotbed of unity. My own branch, the Episcopal Church, grabs headline after headline in the midst of a church-rending fight over human sexuality. As I write these words in the summer of 2007, I read daily of congregations and even dioceses that threaten to leave the church. Tragically, the church seems to be disintegrating before our eyes.

---

1. *Book of Common Prayer* (New York: Oxford University Press, 1979), 359.

The work of forging unity was no easier for the first Christians. Their issues had to do with the basic markers of faith. Who is Jesus? What is his relationship to the Father? What does he accomplish for us in his life, death, and resurrection? What are the conditions under which we enter a covenant relationship with him? Even in Philippians, a letter filled with joy, we find hints—more than hints—that all was not entirely well. Theological and personal conflict threatened the unity of this small and struggling congregation. And so St. Paul devotes much of his second chapter to describing both the importance of unity and the principles that help us to achieve it. "Make my joy complete," Paul pleads (Philippians 2:2), as he urges his friends to discover what binds them together and to commit themselves to the essential task of seeking unity.

CHAPTER 4

One Heart, One Mind

Philippians 2:1–4

"The names have been changed," as the old *Dragnet* show used to say, "to protect the innocent." A clergy friend (let's call him Father Jerry) told me about a devastating conflict in his parish (let's call it St. Willibrord's) on the subject of pews. Yes, pews. The vestry of St. Willibrord's decided that it was time to put genuine pews in the church, after years of sitting on cold, uncomfortable folding chairs. The vestry appointed a subcommittee to investigate the cost and make a report. A few months later, the subcommittee told the vestry that a particular pew company made a product that fit the parish budget. The pews were sturdy and attractive, with sufficient bookrack space for prayer books and hymnals. There was only one item still to be decided: to pad or not to pad? The manufacturer made this pew in a padded (you could choose from several colors for the padding) and an unpadded model. Which, the subcommittee asked, did the vestry prefer?

The ensuing conflict made its way from the vestry (which was too divided to resolve the issue) into the entire congregation. People lined up on both sides. The "pro-pads" asserted that comfortable seating would attract new parishioners and would make worship more livable when the rector lost track of time during his sermons (apparently a frequent occurrence). The "anti-pads," on the other hand, argued that wooden pews, unadorned and simple, are more traditional and certainly more rigorous, a reminder that worship should stretch and challenge us, physically as well as spiritually. Tempers flared. The coffee hour after the Eucharist became tense as parishioners lobbied for their point of view. The vestry, in despair, decided to call a special parish meeting to settle the matter. After a couple of hours of heated debate, the "pro-pads" won, on a 51–49 vote. New pews, pads and all, were quickly installed.

That didn't settle the matter, of course. Some "anti-pads" left the church, taking their pledges with them. Others stayed but continued to mutter. The "pro-pads" didn't make things easier; many seemed to gloat at their victory. One "anti-pad" grandfather, Father Jerry told me, refused to attend his grandson's baptism at St. Willibrord's, announcing that he wouldn't sit down in a pew unless the pads were removed. The whole thing would be comic if it weren't true. Father Jerry said that the conflict dominated his life for months, deflected his attention from mission to damage control, and robbed him of his joy.

With variations only in detail rather than substance, this conflict has been repeated in countless ways down the centuries and around the world. Christians always find something to fight about. And when we fight, the gospel is impaired and our joy evaporates.

Church conflict, incidentally, is never simple or tidy. It's always a complex reality that includes multiple elements and many layers. I have a theory that conflict issues from three sources: principle, personality, and power. But a conflict over principle will almost always include elements of power and personality, even if the latter aren't acknowledged. The conflict at St. Willibrord's, for example, seems at first glance to involve a question of church practice—not quite theological but certainly touching on traditions and customs. A principle is involved, albeit a principle well down the scale from (say) the Nicene Creed. But, in fact, there's no such thing as a dispute centered *purely* on principle. Human nature won't allow it. As conflict heats up, strong personalities engage. Winners and losers emerge. People jockey for power and control, line up votes, seek to defeat the opposition. And, to make things worse, church conflict has now been exacerbated by the Internet. The bread and butter of a bishop's ministry is conflict resolution. Clergy and vestries regularly ask me to intervene when a parish finds itself in an interpersonal tangle. By the time I get involved, however, things have often spun out of control. One person sends an e-mail complaint to another parishioner; the original e-mail is forwarded to ten more who, in turn, pass it on to the entire parish. Even if the original conflict had to do with principle, the Internet quickly transforms it into a confusing jumble of personality, power, and bruised egos.

Tragically, this has been the experience of the church from its earliest days. The disciples, at as solemn a moment as the Last Supper, devolved into conflict. "A dispute also arose among them as to which one of them was to be regarded as the greatest" (Luke 22:24). This conflict doesn't even attempt to masquerade as a matter of principle! More subtly, the early Christians struggled over the question of observing the Jewish law (we'll hear more about that in the introduction to Part III). This was a conflict over principle par excellence. And yet, the New Testament rather frankly presents the personal as well as the theological issues. "When Cephas [Peter] came to Antioch," Paul tells the Christians in Galatia, "I opposed him to his face, because he stood self-condemned; for until certain people came from James, he used to eat with the Gentiles. But after they came, he drew back and kept himself separate for fear of the circumcision faction. And the other Jews joined him in this hypocrisy, so that even Barnabas was led astray by their hypocrisy" (Galatians 2:11–13). Reading these words—even in stately English translation—they fairly sizzle. Yes, the issue was deeply theological. But personality and power had clearly entered in. It took a move of the Spirit, reported in detail in Acts 15, to untangle the mess.

Forging unity is hard work. And so St. Paul begins the second chapter of Philippians by explaining why unity is so important and what makes it possible in the face of our fractious human nature.

"If then there is any encouragement in Christ, any consolation from love, any sharing in the Spirit, any compassion and sympathy, make my joy complete" (2:1–2a). The "if" here is probably rhetorical. Paul lifts up qualities of the Christian life and says in effect, "Since this is true about you, unity should be a primary goal." He tells his friends, to begin with, that Jesus Christ himself encourages us. The word for encouragement, *parakalesis*, is related to a title that the New Testament gives both to Jesus (1 John 2:1—"we have an advocate with the Father") and to the Holy Spirit (John 14:16—"[the Father] will give you another Advocate to be with you forever"). A *parakalesis* is one who comes alongside you and pleads for you; and that, says the New Testament, is what Jesus and the Spirit do for us. Paul goes on to say that we have experienced the consolation of God's love and the sharing (*koinonia*) in the Holy Spirit; the latter word is the same he uses in Philippians 1:5 to describe the partnership we share with one another in the gospel. Finally, he reminds his friends in Philippi that they have experienced both compassion (*splanchna*, which we encountered in 1:8 as a rather visceral depiction of Paul's care for his Philippian friends) and sympathy (*oiktirmoi*, a strong term that refers to pity for the ills of others). All of these phrases, one piled upon another, emphasize that we are the recipients of a whole range of gifts. Jesus encourages us, God's love fills us, the Holy Spirit dwells in us, and we are the beneficiaries of supernatural care. *That*, Paul tells us, is why we should bend our wills and our energies to make his joy complete by striving for unity.

But how are we to accomplish this? Paul lists, in staccato fashion, a series of behavioral challenges. "Be of the same mind, having the same love, being in full accord and of one mind. Do nothing from selfish ambition or conceit, but in humility regard others as better than yourselves. Let each of you look not to your own interests, but to the interests of others" (2:2b–4). Paul could hardly issue a more countercultural directive. He's telling his friends that there's something more important than winning. Unity trumps victory. Your first priority, Paul says, must be to safeguard relationships. Even when principle is involved—and there are indeed occasions when Christians disagree about substantial matters of faith—clarity of truth isn't our only goal. I speak as one who has a definite and rather traditional perspective on the current controversy in the Anglican Communion on the matter of human sexuality. On the theological and political spectrum of the Episcopal Church, I'm a conservative. So Paul's words provide an important corrective for me. Yes, I am a partisan in the conflict. But in the end I must pursue unity as well as truth, as twin and equally binding values. To do less is to dishonor the gospel.

God put me to the test in 2003. That summer, the Episcopal Church's General Convention—the triennial governing body of our church—faced a painful decision. The Diocese of New Hampshire had elected Gene Robinson, a partnered gay man, to be its new bishop. Because of the timing of the election, the canons required the General Convention to give its consent before Gene could be ordained. And so we found ourselves faced with an up or down vote: not simply on the specific bishop-elect, but on the larger question of whether it was appropriate for the church to ordain as bishop a person in a homosexual partnership. The debate was protracted, heated, and *very* public; news media, print and electronic, descended on the Minneapolis Convention Center for what seemed like an ecclesiastical version of the gunfight at the OK Corral. Eventually, of course, Convention gave consent. I spoke and voted with the minority, arguing against the move both on theological grounds and because such a decision would lead inevitably to division and alienation within the church.

When a new bishop-elect receives consent, he or she is invited onto the floor of the House of Bishops and given seat and voice (but not vote; that must await the bishop-elect's ordination, generally some months down the road). And so the day after General Convention had granted consent for Gene's ordination, the Presiding Bishop officially welcomed him, and a group of bishops escorted him onto the floor. My colleagues, all of them (or so it seemed from where I sat), gave him a standing ovation. I hadn't prepared myself for this moment. For the past twenty-four hours, I had struggled with spiritual desolation in the aftermath of the Convention's vote. Do I even belong here?—I found myself asking. Has the church so rejected a traditional understanding of Christian marriage that someone like me doesn't belong here any more? Have I given my priestly and episcopal allegiance to a church that has sold its soul to the Spirit of the Age? Have we rejected Catholic faith and order so thoroughly that we're now on the fringes of the Christian church, rather than the mainstream? And yet, I'd spent my whole Christian life in the Episcopal Church and had bound myself irrevocably to my brothers and sisters. Leaving was (and is) unimaginable. With my head and heart still reeling from these painful thoughts, I heard the Presiding Bishop announce Gene's arrival, and my colleagues jumped to their feet. I didn't move. I sat there, head down, immobilized, and waited for the ovation to finish.

I can hardly remember what transpired on the floor of the House of Bishops over the next couple of hours. My mind played and replayed a kind of mental video of the moment when Gene was escorted into the House and my own refusal to rise. Finally, during a break, I made my way over to Gene's table, introduced myself, and sat down with him. I told him that I had voted no and would do so again if forced to make that terrible decision. And then I confessed that I had failed to "respect the dignity of every human being"[2] and, in particular, *his* dignity, when I refused to stand. Whatever I believe about his election as bishop or the appropriateness of the General Convention's action, he is my brother in Christ. Finally, I told Gene that I would do everything I can to see to it that our relationship glorify Jesus Christ. While in the intervening years I have not changed my mind about these difficult issues—would still, I say with sorrow, vote no—Gene and I are beloved friends and brothers. I praise God for our relationship, and pray that it will be something of a sign of the unity that only Jesus can bring.

American culture values winning. That's not a bad thing, I suppose; it does foster a certain striving for excellence. But the dark side can destroy us and destroy the ones whom we oppose. Paul suggests that there's another way. "Regard others as better than yourselves. Let each of you look not to your own interests, but to the interests of others" (2:3b–4). We must assume that our opponents are acting out of motives as noble as our own, that they too seek God's will, that we might just be wrong. This is tough business, and every cell in our body rebels against it. Paul is telling us that we should not press our case in such a way that it harms people, imperils relationships, or shatters the unity of the Church of God. Even when we're convinced that our opponents are wrong, dead wrong, we must treat them with the utmost respect and operate at every stage with the intention of seeking "the same mind . . . the same love . . . in full accord . . . of one mind" (2:2). That is a call that will demand a lifetime's effort.

I confess an unholy fascination with the *Godfather* saga—the trio of movies that tells the story of the rise and fall of Michael Corleone, head of a large and dangerous crime family. These films, more than any other

---

1. *Book of Common Prayer* (New York: Oxford University Press, 1979), 305.

I know, demonstrate the power of human sin and our helplessness when we try on our own (as Michael does in the final movie) to extricate ourselves. What's missing from the movies, of course, is the grace of the Lord Jesus Christ; but that's another story.

Toward the end of the first film, when Michael is consolidating his leadership, it comes time for him to assume his title, and he will do that by serving as godfather to his sister's child (I should add that he's already ordered the execution of his sister's husband, but that, too, is another story). Michael has also decided to eliminate his Mafia opponents, heads of rival "families," and has dispatched his troops to accomplish the deed. And so the movie jumps back and forth between the baptism and the murders, one by one, of Michael's enemies. During the baptismal liturgy, after Michael has affirmed all of the articles of the Apostles' Creed, the priest asks him, "Do you renounce Satan?" Michael says, "I do renounce him." Cut to a murder—BAM! "And all his works?"—"I do renounce them." Cut to a murder—BAM! "And all his pomps?"—"I do renounce them." Cut to a murder—BAM!

I hesitate to give the *Godfather* the final word in this chapter, but there's an important disincentive here. That terrible climactic scene demonstrates what a spiritual disconnect looks like. Michael believes all the right things. His faith is impeccable. (In the third film, he receives a Papal medal!) But I see in this scene a tragic parable of the church in conflict. We affirm, all of us, what we deeply believe. We may even be right. And yet the way that we consume one another in the church gives the lie to the very faith that we proclaim. At least in our era we don't cut to a murder, though earlier generations of Christians didn't hesitate to do so, on *both* sides of the Reformation, for example. But church conflict—whether it's over a relatively small matter within a congregation or a more sublime and theologically loaded question that's dividing a Christian communion—has the ability to sap our energies, deflect us from what's really important, and (as my friend Father Jerry noted) rob us of our joy.

St. Paul challenges his friends in Philippi, and he challenges us as well, to commit ourselves to finding another way. He's given us a reason for doing it (not least, the gifts that Jesus has already so lavishly poured upon us) and, in the first sentences of Philippians 2, a strategy to accomplish it. The very credibility of our proclamation is at stake.

QUESTIONS FOR REFLECTION

1. How have you experienced conflict in the body of Christ? What effect has it had on your faith?

2. What strategies have you employed to resolve conflict? Were they effective?

3. When you deal with Christians with whom you have significant disagreements, how have you been able to remain in relationship? Or have you?

4. How is the Lord challenging you to seek unity today?

CHAPTER 5

Downward Mobility

Philippians 2:5–11

Anthony Trollope's six-volume *The Chronicles of Barsetshire* tells the story of a fictional English county in the middle of the nineteenth century. A major focus of the saga is the Church of England and its most fallible clerics. The first volume, *The Warden*, for example, highlights a conflict between Archdeacon Grantly and his father-in-law, the most saintly Reverend Septimus Harding. Trollope, throughout "The Chronicles," portrays Grantly as the quintessential ecclesiastical ladder-climber. Over and over, the archdeacon seeks preferment (the old term for an advantageous church appointment) and power. He is portrayed as officious, grasping, and self-important. At a climactic moment toward the end of *The Warden*, Archdeacon Grantly storms out of a meeting with his father-in-law, who has, as a matter of principle, refused to accept the archdeacon's vision of priestly life: "The archdeacon took up his shining new clerical hat, and put on his black new clerical gloves, and looked heavy, respectable, decorous, and opulent, a decided clergyman of the Church of England, every inch of him."[1]

---

1. Anthony Trollope, *The Warden* (1855; London: Penguin Books, 1982), 163–64.

The archdeacon has not, I suspect, read and pondered the second chapter of St. Paul's Letter to the Philippians. He has succumbed instead to a nineteenth-century version of "upward mobility." Paul, on the other hand, paints a very different picture.

In the opening sentences of Philippians 2, St. Paul has been encouraging his friends to "look not to your own interests, but to the interests of others" (2:4). He has been urging, indeed pleading, for the Christian community in Philippi to embrace unity for the sake of the gospel, and his plea is as pertinent today as it was when first written. Now, as the chapter progresses, Paul goes deeper. He moves from an argument that's primarily moral to one that is profoundly theological. He's asking his friends to transform their vision of the Christian life by gazing in wonder at the self-emptying of Jesus himself. Paul's emphasis is not so much on the particulars of Jesus' life and ministry—his teaching and preaching, his healing and miracle-working, the multiplying of loaves and walking on water and raising the dead—as it is on the *meaning* of that life and ministry. Paul tells us that something unimaginable has happened. The God of the Universe has stripped himself, taken off the garments of divinity, and been born as a human being. We find here an early expression of what would later be called the doctrine of the Incarnation: "The word became flesh and lived among us" (John 1:14). Paul makes this point by singing a hymn.

Many biblical scholars believe that the sentences found in Philippians 2:6–11 are, in fact, an early Christian hymn—whether of Paul's composition or someone else's, no one knows. The Greek is rhythmic, and the sentences can be arranged into stanzas. As I mentioned in the prologue, Paul sang, and so did the early Christian Church. So, quite naturally, the words of Christian hymnody would plant themselves in Paul's heart and inevitably make their way into his writing. That seems to be what's happening here. He *sings* his theology, and in doing so has given us a powerful and memorable expression of the heart of the Christian story. Over the centuries, Christians have prayed and pondered these stanzas and have turned them into their own hymns—for example, this hymn by Fortunatus, often sung to Ralph Vaughn Williams' famous tune:

At the name of Jesus
every knee shall bow,
every tongue confess him
King of glory now;
'tis the Father's pleasure
we should call him Lord,
who from the beginning
was the mighty Word.[2]

Before he bursts into song, Paul sets the stage. "Let the same mind be in you that was in Christ Jesus" (Philippians 2:5). In other words, we must allow the Spirit to transform us from the inside out and to do so by reproducing in us the same attitude that we find in Jesus himself. That attitude is the breathtaking surprise at the center of the gospel message: the "downward mobility" of the Son of God. He was enthroned above heaven and earth but let it all go, became a slave, died, and only then was exalted as Lord. If that's what Jesus has done for you, Paul implies, you should be willing to do the same for one another. Paul makes his point by singing a three-part song.

First, the Son was enthroned. "He was in the form of God" (2:6a), Paul says; and "form" translates *morphe*, which points to the Son's very nature. It's fair to say that the technical vocabulary of Trinitarian doctrine—"eternally begotten of the Father, God from God, Light from Light, true God from true God, begotten, not made, of one Being with the Father"[3]—isn't found in the New Testament; but it's also fair to say that one finds in this passage the seed of what would eventually bear fruit in that doctrine: that God eternally exists in three persons, Father, Son, and Holy Spirit. As N. T. Wright has recently argued, Paul places Jesus at the heart of Jewish monotheism:

This passage [Philippians 2:6–11] does indeed express a very early, very Jewish, and very high Christology, in which Paul understands the

---

2. *The Hymnal 1982* (New York: Church Hymnal Corporation,, 1985), Hymn 435.
3. *Book of Common Prayer* (New York: Oxford University Press, 1979), 358.

human being Jesus to be identical with one who from all eternity was equal with the creator God, and who gave fresh expression to what that equality meant by incarnation, humiliating suffering, and death.[4]

Using decidedly Jewish terminology and thought forms, he sees a kind of identity between Jesus and the God of the Hebrew Scriptures; and, over the next few centuries, the church would work out that identity and its meaning in greater and greater detail. We affirm that reflection every time we proclaim the Nicene Creed and every time we celebrate the cycle of feasts that marks the Incarnation—the Annunciation, the Visitation, Christmas, Holy Name Day, Epiphany, and the Presentation—a multipart drama that points to the Word Made Flesh.

Paul is making it clear, before he looks at greater length at the "emptying" of the Son, that the Son occupied a place of exaltation in the presence of the Father and was in the *morphe* of God. In another (and possibly hymnlike) passage, Paul expounds on this point. "He is the image of the invisible God, the firstborn of all creation; for in him all things in heaven and on earth were created, things visible and invisible, whether thrones or dominions or rulers or powers—all things have been created in him and for him. He himself is before all things, and in him all things hold together" (Colossians 1:15–17). Even in the period when the New Testament was written, Christians were looking for ways to express the relationship between Jesus and God, and to find vocabulary that would at once maintain Jewish monotheism and recognize the absolutely unique status of Jesus. St. Paul's Christology is both "high" and poetic, filled with wonder as he struggles for words.

Second, the Son emptied himself. After his brief reference to the place of the preincarnate Christ (obviously, that isn't Paul's terminology), he turns to the crux of the story. The Son, Paul says, "did not regard equality with God as something to be exploited, but emptied himself, taking the form of a slave, being born in human likeness. And being found in human form, he humbled himself and became obedient to the point of death—even death on a cross" (2:6b–8). To begin with,

---

4. N. T. Wright, *Paul: In Fresh Perspective* (Minneapolis: Fortress Press, 2005), 93.

what is Paul getting at when he says that the Son wouldn't "exploit" his equality with God, but rather "emptied himself"? Biblical scholars argue about the precise meaning of Paul's words. What precisely did he give up? His divinity? Not exactly. God, after all, can't stop being God. Perhaps it's better to say that the Son gave up some of the perks of divinity: omniscience, omnipotence, omnipresence, the qualities that he set aside when he took human form. During his earthly ministry, after all, Jesus was neither all-knowing (Mark 13:32), nor all-powerful (Mark 6:5), nor all-present (when he preached at Capernaum, for instance, by definition he wasn't simultaneously preaching in Nazareth). This, of course, is speculation. Not being God ourselves, we may never fully comprehend what the Son laid aside. The mystery of his emptying is just that, a mystery, to be received but perhaps never fully understood. We can only gaze in awe at him who was enthroned above the heavens, yet condescended to become one of us.

Paul adds three key concepts. He tells us, to begin with, that Jesus became a slave. The Greek word (*doulos*) is quite specific about that. Earlier translations tended to tidy up this passage by rendering *doulos* as "servant"; but more recently—in the New Revised Standard Version of the Bible, for example, which we're using in this book—the term is more honestly and painfully translated. The self-emptying of the Son meant that he took the lowest place. For Paul's readers, *doulos* would conjure up an immediate mental image. Slavery was common in the Roman Empire; a huge percentage of the population lived in perpetual bondage. Slaves possessed no rights, did not control their own destinies, and lived at the beck and call of their masters. That's how completely Jesus emptied himself of the privileges of divinity.

Paul goes on to make another and equally startling assertion. He was "born in the human likeness . . . found in human form" (2:7). The Revised English Bible captures these phrases powerfully: "Bearing the human likeness, sharing the human lot, [Jesus] humbled himself." In other words, the self-emptying of the Son is the flip side of Genesis 1. "Then God said, 'Let us make humankind in our image, according to our likeness.' . . . God created humankind in his image, in the image of God he created them; male and female he created them" (Genesis 1:26a, 27). When God called humanity into existence, he intended that we somehow (theologians have argued for millennia about the "how") carry in us a family resemblance to the Almighty God. Tragically, our rebellion has marred that image. And so at the center of God's restoration process is an unimaginable act. God in Christ takes *our* image. He becomes *like us*. As the Letter to the Hebrews puts it, "Since, therefore, the children share flesh and blood, he himself likewise shared the same things. . . . He had to become like his brothers and sisters in every respect" (Hebrews 2:14, 17). God reverses the story of creation and enters into the realm of space and time, fully human and, indeed, a slave.

The third concept is the most painful of all. Jesus "became obedient to the point of death—even death on a cross" (2:8). Like the reality of slavery, crucifixion would have an immediate and graphic reference for Paul's readers in Philippi. It was the Roman Empire's most cruel and public manner of execution, protracted and humiliating. When Jesus urged his disciples to "deny themselves and take up their cross daily and follow me" (Luke 9:23), he was invoking an image that would horrify, perhaps repel, his hearers. Jesus knew what he was doing and so did Paul, as he reminded his friends in Philippi that the self-emptying of Jesus came to a climax on the cross. Like Susan and Lucy at the Stone Table, who turn away their heads as the White Witch slays Aslan,[5] so instinctively we avert our eyes. There is nothing ennobling about an instrument of torture, nothing encouraging about a lifeless corpse nailed to a piece of wood. Yet Paul invites us to turn to Jesus on the cross and to see in his terrible death the most profound sign of God's unfathomable love.

> For me, kind Jesus, was thy incarnation,
> thy mortal sorrow, and thy life's oblation;
> thy death of anguish and thy bitter passion
> for my salvation.[6]

5. C. S. Lewis, *The Lion, the Witch and the Wardrobe* (New York: HarperCollins, 1950), 155.

6. *The Hymnal 1982* (New York: Church Hymnal Corporation, 1985) Hymn 158.

It's always dangerous to include in a book like this an allusion to contemporary culture. What's striking today will soon be forgotten. Yet I find myself thinking about *American Idol*; so I plunge ahead. *American Idol* is television's current version of the rags-to-riches story. The premise is simple. Ordinary people audition before a celebrity panel—singing, dancing, playing an instrument—and the panel eliminates contestant after contestant. Part of the "fun" of the program consists of the offhanded and often cruel dismissal of the losers, who leave the stage with shoulders sagging and brows creased. Finally, after many weeks of auditions, one of these ordinary people is proclaimed the winner. He or she is an idol, a new superstar. This is "upward mobility" at its very best, the American myth unfolding on our television screens. *American Idol* resonates with the American soul.

That's why Paul's hymn is so thoroughly countercultural. At the heart of the gospel story is the "downward mobility" of the Son of God. We must never, Paul reminds us, stray far from the cross.

Finally, the Son is exalted. "Therefore God also highly exalted him and gave him the name above every name, so that at the name of Jesus every knee should bend, in heaven and on earth and under the earth, and every tongue should confess that Jesus Christ is Lord, to the glory of God the Father" (2:9–11). "Highly exalted" is compressed language, referring to Jesus' resurrection from the dead, his ascension to the Father, and his reign over heaven and earth. Jesus has resumed the glory he had laid aside in his incarnation. "Worthy is the Lamb that was slaughtered," cry the angels in heaven, "to receive power and wealth and wisdom and might and honor and glory and blessing" (Revelation 5:12). For "the kingdom of the world has become the kingdom of our Lord and of his Messiah, and he will reign forever and ever" (Revelation 11:15). In that one phrase "highly exalted," the imagery of the Book of Revelation finds concise expression. Jesus reigns. He is "King of kings and Lord of lords" (Revelation 19:16).

All creation, Paul tells us in this hymn, will join heaven's chorus in singing Jesus' praises. We will all someday bow the knee. We will all confess him as Lord. When we do so now, we are anticipating our eternal destiny. I mentioned in Chapter 3 that the first Christian creed was the simple (is it *ever* simple?) affirmation that Jesus is Lord. Paul says that this creed will become the universal cry of all creation. Whenever we affirm the lordship of Jesus, whenever we seek to follow Jesus in the smallest and apparently most undramatic of ways, we are anticipating and perhaps hastening the coming of the Kingdom. Jesus' exaltation, in other words, isn't merely a theoretical expression of faith. It has practical implications today in how we deal with others and how we offer our lives to the Lord.

In the mid-1990s, I found myself (much to my surprise) as a finalist in the election of a bishop suffragan in a diocese in the Deep South. (A "bishop suffragan" is an assistant bishop, one who helps the diocesan bishop to carry out his or her vision. Bishops suffragan do not automatically succeed the diocesan when the latter retires.) A friend had dropped my name into the process, and a series of interviews led to my inclusion in the final slate of nominees. To be honest, I didn't give myself much chance of getting elected. If nothing else, I am distinctly northern. My great-grandfather, James Aloysius Little, rode with General Sheridan during the Shenandoah Valley campaign of 1864, burning and pillaging Virginia farms; and I had a feeling that my northernness would come out every pore, not only in my accent, but also in a whole range of unacknowledged cultural attitudes. Still I entered the election with good humor and a willingness to test the Spirit to see if this was indeed God's call.

Obviously it wasn't. The diocese happily elected one of its own, and he has been a superb and supportive colleague to the diocesan bishop and, since my own election in Northern Indiana, a valued brother in the House of Bishops. But God did have something to teach me, and in a surprising way.

Two weeks before the election, the five finalists came together to answer questions in the presence of clergy and lay persons who would eventually select the next bishop suffragan. I will never forget the scene. The nominees sat at a table in front of two or three hundred "voters." A member of the diocesan standing committee (a governing body of the diocese) posed a series of questions, five of them. All of the nominees, according to the rules of the meeting, would answer all five questions; and each nominee would take a turn at being first up. Most of the questions, of course, were quite predictable. What is your vision for congregational development? What most excites you about this diocese? Inevitably, one of the questions dealt with an issue that has dominated our lives for decades: Would you bless a same-sex union? Why or why not? The most intriguing question came at the end, in the form of a request: please share with us a biblical passage that summarizes your ministry, and tell us why it does so. In almost a single motion, five black-suited men reached into their suit jackets and drew out New Testaments. I quickly settled on 1 Corinthians 2:2: "For I decided to know nothing among you except Jesus Christ and him crucified."

The Holy Spirit, apparently, had other plans. To my horror, the candidate who spoke immediately before me chose the same 1 Corinthians passage. And so, with virtually no lead time, and in the presence of several hundred "voters," I searched my memory for a passage that would summarize my life and my work as a priest. 1 Peter 4:11 suddenly popped into my head: "so that God may be glorified in all things through Jesus Christ. To him belong the glory and the power forever and ever. Amen." This turned out to be one of those occasions (I'll mention another in the next chapter) when I found myself preaching a sermon that I hadn't anticipated. What came out (in brief) was something like this:

The goal of my life and my ministry, I heard myself saying, is to glorify Jesus, and that's a tough challenge indeed. It's especially hard for clergy. People lionize us and put us on a pedestal, and the danger for me—and for all of my brothers in front of you—is that we're tempted to think that it's actually true. There is really nothing more unhelpful than for someone to pass by in the line at the end of a service and say, "Wonderful sermon, Father!" I love to hear this, of course; the clerical ego exults in praise. But how much more appropriate if the greeter had said, "Wonderful Lord we have, Father!" *That*, after all, is what preaching and teaching and celebrating the sacraments and offering pastoral care is all about: lifting up the Lord Jesus. On my tombstone, I said (surprising even myself!), I hope that 1 Peter 4:11 is inscribed—"so that God may be glorified in all things through Jesus Christ." You and I have nothing else to offer to the world. It's all about Jesus.

My speech didn't get me elected (and a good thing, too; the priest they chose was precisely the person the diocese needed); but it did remind me why the Father created me, why Jesus redeemed me, and why the Holy Spirit sanctifies me: to glorify the name of Jesus. It was a Philippians 2 moment. The Father has highly exalted Jesus, and he invites us to join in the praise that all creation offers to the Son. Paul's emphasis on the unity of the church finds its fullest and deepest rationale in the story of redemption—the story of the Son of God who was enthroned, who emptied himself, and who is now most highly exalted. *That*, Paul says, is what Jesus has done for us; and that story should forever transform our attitude toward our brothers and sisters.

QUESTIONS FOR REFLECTION

1. How has our culture's concern for "upward mobility" impacted your vision of Christian life and ministry?

2. How would "downward mobility" express itself in your life, in your work, in your ministry? How would it affect your relationships in the body of Christ?

3. Who in your life has most powerfully lived out the self-emptying that Paul describes in the hymn in Philippians 2?

4. What scripture verse would you like to see inscribed on your tombstone?

CHAPTER 6

Synergy

Philippians 2:12–13

BUT *HOW?*

St. Paul has just spent the first half of Philippians 2 explaining why unity is so important. He urges his friends to apply themselves to healing divisions in the body of Christ, and he cites the life, death, and resurrection of Jesus as the motive for doing so. His case is powerful and compelling. But the history of the church for two millennia makes it clear that the task is virtually impossible. On the contrary, for two thousand years—beginning in the era of the New Testament itself—Christians have struggled with one another and have consistently failed to achieve unity. The legacy of that struggle is found in the thousands of denominations (quite literally—thousands!) that lay claim to being genuine expressions of the church. Our divisions bring scandal to the gospel we proclaim and hamper our ability to commend the faith. And so the question that we face is, *How?* After centuries of failure, how can Christians not only seek unity but actually find it? The task is both daunting and discouraging.

Perhaps the most important and the most overlooked word in the Bible is "therefore." Because we often read the scriptures in devotional snippets, we don't notice the connective tissue that links one section to another. For example, Paul begins Romans 12 with the words, "I appeal to you, therefore. . . . " The "therefore" refers to everything that's gone before it: Paul's grim depiction of the power of sin, God's intervention in Jesus, the faith that binds us to God's actions and restores us to a relationship with the Father, the power of the Holy Spirit to transform us, and the work of God in history. Since God has done all of that, *therefore*, "present your bodies as a living sacrifice" (Romans 12:1). The ethical teaching of the last five chapters of Romans rests firmly on the careful, even tortured, writing found in the first eleven. The same principle holds true in Philippians, though not quite on the grand scale of Romans. Paul begins 2:12 with a "therefore," and he's pointing back to everything he has just written. Unity must be your first priority, he's saying, as Jesus' example compels us to make it so. "*Therefore*, my beloved, just as you have always obeyed me, not only in my presence, but much more now in my absence" (2:12a; italics mine).

Paul goes on to map out a two-point program for unity, a program that's essentially synergistic. What is synergy? It has to do with two forces working together in cooperation. (*Syn* is the Greek word for "with," and *energeia* is, not surprisingly, the root of our word "energy.") Imagine, for example, a five-year-old learning to write the alphabet. (I may be dating myself here, since children seem to learn these skills at younger and younger ages.) She grasps the pencil and places the point on the wide-ruled paper. But she can't quite trace out the letters, and she holds the pencil awkwardly, four fingers on one side, thumb in the other direction (rather than placing the pencil between the index and middle finger). So her parent places a hand over the child's hand. Now, two hands hold the pencil. And the parent and child together begin to write out the alphabet: A, B, C, D . . . Who's writing? The parent or the child? The answer, obviously, is *both*. You can't really separate the two. The child holds the pencil (albeit awkwardly), the parent guides the child's hand, and the alphabet won't end up on paper without both working together. That's synergy: two forces working in cooperation to accomplish a task.

And this is what Paul is describing in our passage. "Therefore . . . work out your own salvation with fear and trembling; for it is God who is at work in you, enabling you both to will and to work for his good pleasure" (2:12–13). How do we obtain the unity that he has been urging on his friends in Philippi? Is it our job or God's? The answer is *both*. When we cooperate wholeheartedly with God's purposes, God accomplishes in us "far more than all we can ask or imagine" (Ephesians 3:20).

The first half of the equation has to do with our effort. "Work out your own salvation with fear and trembling," Paul tells his Philippian friends. The phrase "work out" translates a Greek verb that has at its root *energeia*, a reminder that Paul is talking about significant exertion. This is a marathon, not a leisurely stroll. What exactly do we work out? Our own salvation, Paul says. We need to linger over this phrase and get a sense of what Paul does and doesn't mean. First of all, salvation is a rich biblical concept that means more than the popular understanding of the word. Typically, people both in and beyond the Christian community think of salvation in terms of "going to heaven." The question, "Are you saved?" would mean something like, "Have you done what you need to do, so that when you die you won't go to hell, but rather to heaven?" Now, there's nothing wrong (in fact, there's much right!) with the question, and our eternal dwelling place is, indeed, no small matter. The New Testament of salvation includes that and much more.

Salvation (the Greek word is *soteria*) refers not simply to avoiding hell but also to God's intention for our lives. At times, the New Testament uses the word to refer to physical wholeness. "Come and lay your hands on [my daughter]," Jairus pleads with Jesus, "so that she may be made well, and live" (Mark 5:23). The phrase "made well" translates the verb form of *soteria*. In this case, the wholeness desired is physical. At other times, salvation means most clearly our rescue from sin and its dreadful consequence, death. "There is salvation in no one else," Peter and John tell the religious leaders in Jerusalem, "for there is no other name [the name of Jesus] under heaven given among mortals by which we must be saved" (Acts 4:12). Salvation can point to a past event in which the gospel took root in our lives: "When the goodness and loving kindness of God our Savior appeared, he saved us, not because of any works of righteousness that we had done, but according to his mercy, through the water of rebirth and renewal by the Holy Spirit" (Titus 3:4–5). It can remind us of what the Lord is doing in our lives right now: "To us who are being saved, [the message of the cross] is the power of God" (1 Corinthians 1:18). And it can comfort us about the future, when our rescue from sin and death will be complete: "For salvation is nearer to us now than when we became believers; the night is far gone, the day is near" (Romans 13:11b–12a). A Christian can truthfully say, "I have been saved. I am being saved. I shall be saved."

Paul is not telling his friends in Philippi that they create their own salvation—far from it. God in Christ has already done that. No, he's reminding them that their job is to live out the implications that salvation imposes upon them, to grow into their salvation. Since they've been saved (and are being saved and will be saved), they must undertake to fulfill certain obligations. Chief among them is the quest for unity. They must bend heart, mind, soul, and will to this task, and he uses two words to emphasize how grave is the quest. "Work out your own salvation," he says, "with fear and trembling" (2:12). Fear (the Greek root is *phobos*, root of our word "phobia") and trembling (*tromos*, root of "tremor") point to the seriousness of our mission. We mustn't undertake it lightly. Aslan rightly inspires an appropriate dread: "He's wild, you know. Not like a *tame* lion."[1] And so Paul lays upon the church in Philippi and upon the church in the twenty-first century, the solemn and indeed awesome responsibility to find a way to be "in full accord and of one mind" (Philippians 2:3), not simply for our own sake, but for the sake of the world for which Jesus died.

Now, back to the summer of 2003 and the immediate aftermath of the Episcopal Church's General Convention. My own diocese, like dioceses all around the country, was in turmoil. Every time I hit the download button on my computer, dozens of e-mails would appear in my inbox—day after day, week after week. Some were appalled by what the convention had done. Others were appalled by how I'd voted. What we now call "snail mail" came in at an equally overwhelming rate, with an equal spread of opinion. It seemed that everyone was angry,

---

1. C. S. Lewis, *The Lion, the Witch and the Wardrobe* (New York: HarperCollins, 1950), 182.

and there was no "middle way" that could cut between the unavoidable extremes of yes on Gene or no on Gene. The canons (the official rules and regulations of the church) had not permitted that option.

Among the postal mail was a letter from a man I'll call Bill. He was furious that I'd voted no—because, he told me, he has a gay son whom he loves and supports. Bill saw my vote as a judgment on his son, and he branded me as "hate-filled" and "bigoted." I wrote back as mildly as I could, thanking him for his letter and commending him for supporting his son. I went on to say that I'm committed to welcoming gay and lesbian people into the church but that, tragically, the General Convention had gone a step further. It had required a vote that, I believed, was essentially doctrinal. My conscience had allowed me no course of action than to vote no. But, I concluded, I want to find a way that he and I and his son could be part of the same church, living in the ambiguity created by an issue with no easy resolution. While we might disagree about the church's actions, Jesus calls us into relationship with one another.

I didn't know if my letter satisfied him, but I soon found out. In the weeks following Convention, I convened a series of meetings around the diocese—to give people a chance to hear what had actually happened and to ask whatever questions burned in their hearts and minds. At the first of those meetings, toward the end of the question-and-answer time, Bill stood up. I recognized him at once. The Diocese of Northern Indiana is small enough that, over the course time, names and faces get planted in my mind. Bill said, "Bishop!" (I wish I could reproduce the anger in his voice. My title sounded like an unpleasant expletive.) "Didn't Jesus say, 'Love one another'?" My response turned into another impromptu sermon, like the one I referred to in the last chapter. One could say that I heard myself preaching, heard words coming out of my mouth that were more for me than for Bill.

You're absolutely right, Bill, I told him, Jesus did tell us to love one another. But let's think for a minute about the context of that command. It was at the Last Supper. Jesus had just finished washing the feet of his friends. And then he says, "I give you a new commandment, that you love one another. Just as I have loved you, you also should love one another. By this everyone will know that you are my disciples, if you have love for one another" (John 13:34–35). (I was surprised, looking up the passage later, that the biblical quote came out unaided and almost completely verbatim.) This may be the hardest thing Jesus ever said. I would prefer it if he'd told his disciples, "By this everyone will know that you are my disciples, if you recite the Nicene Creed . . . or if you sign a pledge card." But he didn't do that. Jesus invites the world outside the church to make its judgment about the reality of our claim to be disciples on the basis of how we treat each other. That's terrifying, isn't it? It certainly frightens me. How I deal with you and with gay and lesbian people, and how you deal with folks like me, is going to be primary data for non-Christians. If they see us destroying one another, they'll reject us, and they may well reject Jesus. On the other hand, if they see us taking the risk of being in relationship with one another, they'll know that we're the genuine article. They'll know that our claim to be disciples is authentic. So this painful moment in the life of the church presents, surprisingly, an evangelistic opportunity. If we get this thing right, we might actually draw people to Jesus.

Whatever effect my sermonette had on Bill, I know that it helped me to reframe this difficult time. Don't get me wrong: I would much prefer that we were not consumed by this energy-draining, time-consuming, and probably irresolvable conflict over human sexuality. It is the subtext of the Episcopal Church and of the Anglican Communion in our day. But I can't do anything about that. We don't get to choose the era in which we live or the issues with which we must grapple. And so the question we're facing as a Christian community is not *whether* we disagree about these matters but *how* we do so. St. Paul invites us to look for another way, marked by deep commitment to one another and encouraged by the example of the One who emptied himself and took the form of a slave. It's a task that is worth the investment of our energy, our time, and our very hearts.

The second half of the equation has to do with God's effort. "For it is God," Paul says, "who is at work in you, enabling you both to will and to work for his good pleasure" (2:13). Again, the "at work" comes from a verb based on *energeia*. Something supernatural is going on. His hand grasps our hand, directs the pencil, and makes it possible for our untrained fingers to write the alphabet. In the face of human division,

God works in us and through us to build bridges, tear down walls, and allow us to see Jesus in the most unlikely people. How does he do that? To start with, he prays for us. At the Last Supper, when the meal and the foot washing and the long discourse reported in John 13–16 are done, Jesus intercedes for us with a prayer that's often called the High Priestly Prayer because of its solemn and almost liturgical character. One can imagine Jesus praying this prayer in heaven, as he stands as our great High Priest in the presence of the Father (see Hebrews 5:8–10; 7:25.) It's a prayer for the disciples in the room with him and more: "I ask not only on behalf of these [disciples]," Jesus prays, "but also on behalf of those who will believe in me through their word" (John 17:20)—in other words, for *us*. And his prayer is specifically for unity, that "they may all be one. As you, Father, are in me and I am in you, may they also be in us, so that the world may believe that you have sent me . . . that they may become completely one, so that the world may know that you have sent me" (John 17:21, 23). Our unity is so important to Jesus that he makes it the focus of his final prayer for us. More than that, he puts his own credibility on the line. The world will reject or accept him on the basis of what they see in us. If we display unity, those beyond the Christian community will come to "believe that [the Father] has sent me." If we don't, they will reject not only the church but also Jesus himself. And so Jesus is praying for us, that we will tear down the inevitable barriers that arise in any community. That he is praying means that we do not go about this work unaided.

Jesus' prayer is complemented by a promise. "Apart from me," he also says at the Last Supper, "you can do nothing" (John 15:5). This startling statement falls in the middle of a section in which Jesus is describing our relationship with him in terms of vine and branches. He, of course, is the vine, and we are connected to him as the branches, which draw life and sustenance from him. We are utterly dependent. But that very dependence carries the promise of empowerment. When we recognize how much we need him and when we cry out for wisdom beyond our own, he is most eager to respond. J. B. Phillips, author and translator of the New Testament, points out that something unique happens when we call on the name of Jesus.

A man may find difficulty in writing a poem, but if he cries, "Oh, William Shakespeare, help me!" nothing whatever happens. A man may be terribly afraid, but if he cries, "Oh, Horatio Nelson, help me!" there is no sort of reply. But if he is at the end of his moral resources or cannot by effort of will muster up sufficient positive love and goodness and he cries, "Oh, Christ, help me!" something happens at once. The sense of spiritual reinforcement, of drawing spiritual vitality from a living source, is so marked that Christians cannot help being convinced that their Hero is far more than an outstanding figure of the past.[2]

Jesus promises to empower us (Luke 24:49; Acts 1:8), and Paul has experienced that empowerment (1 Corinthians 2:4; 2 Corinthians 12:9) at times of crisis in his life. We can anticipate no less. Our God is a God of power and surprise. (More about that in the next chapter.) Paul is telling us that when we act, God acts; or, to be precise, we act and God acts at the same time, a single and seamless joining of his energy and ours. The miracle that emerges makes Paul's joy complete (Philippians 2:2) and forges supernatural unity.

QUESTIONS FOR REFLECTION

1. Where in your life do you most need to seek unity, to build bridges? At home, at work, in your church, or in some other setting?

2. What is the necessary step that you must take to build bridges? How might you stretch yourself for the sake of the other?

3. How do you resist?

4. Can you think of a time when you experienced Jesus acting supernaturally in your life? What are the marks or signs of Jesus' presence in your life?

---

2. J. B. Phillips, *Your God Is Too Small* (1952; New York: Touchstone, 2004), 113–14.

CHAPTER 7

Light and Darkness

Philippians 2:14–18

Sometime in the early 1980s—I'm unable to be more precise than that; the details have faded from corporate memory—Enoch Christopherson visited Bakersfield. Mr. Christopherson had something of a dual vocation: he was mayor of Turlock, California, about 150 miles north of Bakersfield, and simultaneously a traveling Pentecostal preacher. And so the phone rang one Saturday night in the home of Father John Keester, rector of All Saints Episcopal Church, and Mr. Christopherson announced that God had directed him to preach at All Saints on Sunday. Father John did not immediately agree to Mr. Christopherson's request (or was it a demand?). Instead, he phoned several parishioners, sought their wisdom, and finally decided that God may have a surprise or two in mind. He called Mr. Christopherson back and gave him permission to preach the next morning.

No one remembers the details of Enoch Christopherson's sermon. It hadn't occurred to anyone to tape the sermon or to take notes. All that remains, a quarter century later, is a recollection that Enoch Christopherson declared that God had called All Saints to be a "lighthouse in the southwest." ("Southwest" *what*? Southwest Bakersfield? The southwestern United States? That wasn't clear.) On the basis of this experience, however, the parish became even more intentional about outreach and mission. Since All Saints' founding in 1967, under the leadership of Father George Woodgates, it had been a mission-oriented congregation, giving away small amounts of money every week (money beyond the obligatory "assessment" owed to the diocese), with a focus on various mission organizations. After Mr. Christopherson's sermon, however, the flame burned hotter. When the parish sold its property and moved deeper into burgeoning southwest Bakersfield, the vestry took 10 percent of the proceeds (about $100,000, no small sum in the early 1980s), put it in an outreach fund, and gave it away. The parish also decided that 10 percent of every Sunday's receipts (beyond the obligatory diocesan "assessment") was to be put into the same fund and given away.

By the time I arrived at All Saints in 1986, the "lighthouse prophecy" (as the sermon came to be known) had planted itself in the parish lore. People talked about it a good deal, but beyond disbursing funds (itself an unusual and financially courageous step), parishioners wondered what lighthouse ministry actually looked like. For the next thirteen years or so, we experimented. The parish dispatched mission teams to do ministry around the diocese—and eventually around the world (to nations as diverse as Uganda, Honduras, India, Uruguay, Argentina, Kenya, and the Dominican Republic). Many parishioners involved themselves in a diverse spectrum of ministries within the city of Bakersfield; others took on leadership positions in the diocese. This small congregation (Sunday attendance never grew much beyond two hundred during my tenure) made a major impact on the world around it. To symbolize our ongoing awareness of the lighthouse prophecy, a parishioner made a huge banner, which hung in the back of the church. The banner displayed a lighthouse, and underneath were words of Jesus from the Sermon on the Mount: "Let your light shine before others, so that they may see your good works and give glory to your Father in heaven" (Matthew 5:16).

Then, in late 1999, God, in his humor, intervened in my life, and I was elected Bishop of Northern Indiana. (Prior to my election, I had set foot in the state of Indiana only three times. Even now I look back on the events of 1999 with wonder, awe, and great surprise.) By accident of calendar—or divine providence—Bishop John-David Schofield was scheduled to make his official visitation to All Saints the Sunday after my election; a fortuitous coincidence, too: my head was dizzy, disoriented by the amazing thing that had happened to me, and I don't think I could have been coherent that morning. As Bishop John-David stood to preach, he looked at me and said, "Ed, at the beginning of the procession this morning, I was noticing the banner at the back of the church. By any chance do you know what's on the seal of the Diocese of Northern Indiana?" No, I said, I don't. (I've never been a connoisseur of diocesan insignia, so I hadn't bothered to check.) Bishop John-David said, "*It's a lighthouse.*"

Indeed, it is. When the diocese came into existence in 1898, the first cathedral was located in Michigan City, Indiana—on the northwest "coast" of the state, along the shore of Lake Michigan. Then and now, Michigan City boasts a beautiful lighthouse on a jetty thrusting out into the lake. Thus, the lighthouse on the diocesan seal was a reminder of the Northern Indiana's origins. (Below the lighthouse, by the way, are words in Greek from John 1:4: *ho phos ton anthropon*, [the light of all people].) Every time I look at the episcopal ring on my right hand, inscribed with the seal of the diocese, a whole array of images passes through my mind: of the lighthouse banner and the lighthouse prophecy that inspired it; of faithful men and women—in Bakersfield and other parishes I've served, and in the Diocese of Northern Indiana—who have taken Jesus so seriously that they've stepped out courageously in mission; of the Apostle Paul himself and his challenge to the Christians in Philippi. They are, he tells them, to "shine like stars in the world" (Philippians 2:15).

Something about us, Paul is saying, should reflect (however imperfectly) the light of Jesus himself.

As he concludes the section of the letter that reflects on unity as a source of joy, Paul turns to the theme of light and darkness. "Do all things without murmuring and arguing," he writes (2:14). Throughout the Bible, grumbling is often portrayed as the source of division. Shortly after the miraculous events at the Red Sea, the Israelites murmur against Moses. "Give us water to drink," they complained. "Why did you bring us out of Egypt, to kill us and our children and our livestock with thirst?" (Exodus 17:2b, 3b). The early Christian church experienced its share of grumbling as well. "Now during those days, when the disciples were increasing in number, the Hellenists [Greek-speaking Christians] complained against the Hebrews [Aramaic-speaking Christians] because their widows were being neglected in the daily distribution of food" (Acts 6:1). Paul's directive in 2:14 indicates that his friends in Philippi were themselves not immune from the tendency to grumble. The answer, he says, is to shine like stars.

What makes this possible? Paul asks the Philippians to remember two things.

First, he reminds them who they are, their *identity*. "Do all things without murmuring and arguing," he says. To what end? "[S]o that you may be blameless and innocent, children of God without blemish in the midst of a crooked and perverse generation" (2:14–15). The phrase I'm highlighting here is "children of God"—which may be the most radical teaching found in the New Testament. All of us are creatures of God. He made us in his image (Genesis 1:26); he loves us beyond our ability to fathom (John 3:16); he knows us better than we know ourselves (Matthew 10:29–30); and he yearns for us to be in relationship with him for ever (1 Timothy 2:4).

But the New Testament goes on to say that Jesus offers us even more. He invites us to become children of God, to enter into a relationship with the Father that is one of "family connection." "To all who received [Jesus], who believed in his name, he gave power to become children of God, who were born, not of blood or of the will of the flesh or of the will of man, but of God" (John 1:12–13). Paul often describes this phenomenon in terms of adoption. "He destined us for adoption as his children through Jesus Christ, according to the good pleasure of his will" (Ephesians 1:5). In other words, the Father gazes at us with the same love that he lavishes upon his Only-Begotten. (My eldest child is adopted, and the experience of adoptive parenthood has given this New Testament teaching a certain reality. Gregory is no less my son because he came to us through adoption. He is *family*.) The Episcopal Church's baptismal liturgy makes the same point: "We receive you into the household of God," the congregation says to the newly baptized.[1]

---

1. *Book of Common Prayer* (New York: Oxford University Press, 1979), 308.

We have been made *family*, children of the Father and brothers and sisters of Jesus.

More than that, we are children of God "without blemish" (2:15). The Greek here stresses an important point that's invisible in English. *Amoma* is a technical term. In the Greek translation of the Old Testament called the *Septuagint*, the word is used to describe animal sacrifices. When you present a bull or a goat in the temple, it's to be without blemish. The New Testament transfers the same term to Jesus himself. *He* is an offering without blemish (Hebrews 9:14; 1 Peter 1:19). And that, Paul tells his friends in Philippi, is the kind of self-offering that they too need to make. Relationships made whole glorify the Lord and are congruent with our status as children of God.

The movie *Joyeux Noelle* tells the story of an incident on the first Christmas Eve of World War I—that is, December 24, 1914. The incident itself actually happened, though the film adds its own dramatic (and melodramatic) elements. The Great War in Western Europe had by then degenerated into trench warfare. Opposing trenches stretched from Belgium into France, and, periodically, one side would assault the other, with no significant exchange of territory. As *Joyeux Noelle* begins, a German unit guards the trench on one side; across from them are French and Scottish units. In between, "no man's land," several hundred yards littered with the debris of war: discarded weapons, unexploded shells, frozen bodies—a grim and heartless moonscape stripped of plant life.

On the German side, a tenor begins to sing "Silent Night." His voice carries easily to the opposing trenches in the clear and cloudless darkness. Across the way, a Scotsman picks up his bagpipe and starts to accompany the German singer. The French troops join in, singing in their own language. Soon the night is filled with the sound of praise rising from the trenches. Then—slowly, reluctantly, fearfully—the troops begin to emerge from their protective ditches and meet in no-man's-land. At first they eye one another suspiciously; but eventually, the barriers come down. A priest (he happens to be a Scot) conducts a worship service in the midst of the debris, surrounded by enemies who had discovered that they are really brothers in Christ, children of the same Father, loved by the same Lord. In the aftermath of this Christmas

Eve truce, the opposing units refuse to resume killing one another and, eventually, their commanding officers have to move them to other sectors of the trench line.

That's what happens, both the film and St. Paul tell us, when we realize who we are. It not only transforms us from the inside out; it also reshapes our relationships.

Second, Paul reminds his friends in Philippi that God has placed a great gift in their care, their *vocation* as Christ's ambassadors. "It is by your holding fast to the word of life," he tells them, "that I can boast on the day of Christ that I did not run in vain or labor in vain" (2:16). The "word of life" points to the proclamation we looked at in Chapter 2, good news of the life, death, and resurrection of Jesus Christ. The Greek language, incidentally, has two words for "life." One is *bios* (which has to do with the life shared by everything that lives, from one-celled amoebae to the most complex of all creatures, human beings), the root of our word "biology." The other Greek word is *zoe*, which refers to life with meaning, depth, purpose, a qualitative assessment. This is the word that the New Testament uses in the phrase "eternal life," and it's the word that Paul employs here. The "word of life" doesn't simply help us to live longer. Rather, it enriches our lives. We're different because we've encountered it. We're different because we've encountered *him*.

In his First Letter to the Corinthians, Paul talks about our responsibility toward the word. We are, he says, "servants of Christ and stewards of God's mysteries" (1 Corinthians 4:1). God has entrusted something precious to us. He has given us a message to commend to the world, and that very message is what binds us together. C. S. Lewis, in his book *Mere Christianity*, says that there is a basic core of belief shared by all Christians (this is what he means by "mere Christianity"). It's not denominationally specific. This is not to say that denominational teaching isn't important or doesn't need to be addressed. But "mere Christianity" refers to that vast foundation of doctrine that all Christians hold in common, the very heart of the faith. It lifts up the essential elements of faith Christians hold in common: who Jesus is, what he's done for us, and how we understand the nature of God to be Triune. "The best, perhaps the only, service I could do for my unbelieving neighbors," Lewis says, "was to explain and defend the belief that has been common to nearly all Christians at all times."[2] That is what Paul is getting at when he uses the phrase the "word of life"; that is the gospel for which we are stewards, to offer to a needy world.

My friend Howard called me one day and asked if I'd be interested in an ecumenical conversation with three Amish bishops. Large sections of the territory included in the Diocese of Northern Indiana have been settled by Christians from the Anabaptist tradition—Mennonites (of various stripes; there's quite a variety), members of the Church of the Brethren and the Missionary Church, and (most dramatically) the Amish. Howard works for the Red Cross blood bank in a county with a large Amish population, and over the years he's come to know and appreciate that unique Christian community. So he called and invited me to join him for an afternoon's discussion with three Amish bishops he'd gotten to know over the years. (The Amish don't have "professional" seminary-trained clergy common in other churches; their bishops are, in essence, the unpaid—in the Episcopal Church we'd say "bi-vocational"—pastors of local congregations, assisted by two other ordained orders: what they call "the ministry" and deacons.) My first reaction to Howard's invitation, to be honest, was negative. The Amish live in another century, and in this case that's not simply a figurative comment. I couldn't imagine that we could find enough in common to sustain a genuine dialogue.

Finally, albeit reluctantly, I agreed. The day for our discussion arrived. We were to meet in a church in the South Bend area, with Howard driving his Amish friends to the gathering. (The Amish are not permitted to drive automobiles; but they can travel in them, as long as an English—their word for non-Amish—drives the vehicle.) I arrived at the church first and waited in the parking lot for my ecumenical partners to arrive. When Howard and his friends drove up in Howard's minivan, the three Amish bishops emerged and we stood for a moment in silence, each (I'm sure) horrified by the other. To me, they looked as though they'd stepped from a time machine, in their flat-brimmed hats and buttonless coats, beards long and squared off. To them, I must have

---

2. C. S. Lewis, *Mere Christianity* (1952; New York: Collier Books, 1960), 6.

looked equally strange, bedecked in magenta, amethyst ring and gold pectoral chain gleaming in the sun, their nightmare of medieval prelacy. Howard ushered us into the church, and the dialogue began.

For the first hour or so, the conversation was predictably awkward. We nibbled at the edge of each other's lives. I wondered what it's like to live without electricity, the Internet, running water, and (I had to be delicate about this) indoor plumbing. They, of course, asked questions about life when you actually have these modern conveniences. We also talked about the church and its worship, though the discussion tended to focus on the superficial: how long services can last (the Amish have amazing liturgical endurance—three hours for a typical Sunday service, six hours when the Lord's Supper is celebrated), who gets to preach, how officers are chosen or elected. As things began to wind down (more accurately, to sputter out), the Amish bishop named Samuel said, "I have a gift for you." He handed me an Amish prayer book. I was surprised, of course, to find that the Amish actually employ a simple liturgy (I'd assumed that their worship would be completely spontaneous). The prayer book was printed in two languages, Pennsylvania Dutch (really an old form of German) on one page, English facing it on the other. As I thumbed through the prayer book, I stumbled upon a surprise.

"Why, you've got the Apostles Creed in here!" I said, almost incredulously.

"Yes, of course," Samuel replied. "Do you have it, too?"

"You bet!" I said.

"But do you actually *believe* it?" Samuel asked.

"You bet!" I said again. "Every single word."

And at that moment something miraculous happened, the divine half of the synergy that I talked about in the last chapter. Suddenly, unexpectedly, we saw one another with fresh eyes. We discerned, despite the vast difference in culture and language and experience, that we were brothers in Christ. The atmosphere in the room changed. The Holy Spirit opened our hearts. Just as the disciples on the road to Emmaus knew the risen Lord in the breaking of the bread (Luke 24:31), so we recognized the presence of the risen Jesus in one another. That's what St. Paul is getting at when he urges his friends in Philippi to continue "holding fast to the word of life" (2:16). When we do, barriers fall.

Paul ends this section by returning to the theme of joy. "But even if I am being poured out as a libation over the sacrifice and the offering of your faith, I am glad and rejoice with all of you—and in the same way you also must be glad and rejoice with me" (2:17–18). Stuck in the stocks in an unknown prison, he remembers that Jesus has bound the Philippian Christians to Jesus—and to one another. The memory fills him with joy.

QUESTIONS FOR REFLECTION

1. Paul's warning about "murmuring and arguing" has a painfully contemporary feel. How do you deal with that tendency in your own life?

2. How do you articulate your identity as a Christian and as a child of God? What is distinctively Christian?

3. How is Jesus challenging you to hold the word of life—and to pass it on?

4. How has God surprised you by enabling you to see the presence of Jesus in unexpected persons or situations?

PART III

Confidence in Jesus

"Finally, my brothers and sisters, rejoice in the Lord. To write the same things to you is not troublesome to me, and for you it is a safeguard" (Philippians 3:1). St. Paul's "finally" is perhaps a bit premature! He still has got two chapters to go and much ground still to cover. But before he does so, he again reminds his friends in Philippi that joy permeates everything he says. With that reminder, he turns to a difficult topic.

I mentioned in Chapter 4 that the early church struggled with the question of the relationship between Christian faith and the Jewish law, in particular the law's ceremonial requirements (circumcision, a kosher kitchen, and Sabbath observance, among other items). Were these requirements binding on Gentiles who wished to follow Jesus? Were they marks of the New Covenant as well as the Old? Paul's clear answer was no, but the battle raged throughout his life and ministry and manifested itself in settings as diverse as Rome, Galatia, Antioch, Jerusalem, and Philippi. And so he says, "Beware of the dogs, beware of the evil workers, beware of those who mutilate the flesh" (3:2). This is a rather sarcastic reference to circumcision, a practice that marked male members of the Covenant community from the time of the patriarch Abraham (Genesis 17:10–14). In an era before anesthesia, the question of circumcision was pressing indeed, and a significant issue for those who pondered the cost of discipleship. Elsewhere, Paul is even more derisive about the practice. "I wish that those who unsettle you [by requiring circumcision] would castrate themselves!" he tells the

Christians in Galatia (Galatians 5:12). Many translations soften this difficult phrase.

Paul's purpose in Philippians 3, however, is not simply to mock those who advocate circumcision. Instead, it's to ask the question from another perspective. What *can* give us confidence that we belong to Jesus, that we're included in the Covenant? If it isn't the ceremonial law, what is it? He gives three answers over the course of several paragraphs. We know Jesus. We're growing in Jesus. And we can be confident that Jesus has an eternal destiny for us. These too yield a harvest of joy, even in the face of the most painful circumstances.

CHAPTER 8

Knowing Jesus

Philippians 3:3–11

When I was fifteen, my cousin Joe invited me to be an usher at his wedding. This was the first time (and, it turned out, the *only* time) that I was accorded such an honor. The wedding itself was something of a blur. As a thoroughly unchurched person (still several years away from my Christian conversion), I was unfamiliar with religious ceremony; and so I missed the significance of much of the service. During the reception that followed, though, I was in more familiar territory, schmoozing with relatives, eating, looking with envy at those old enough to drink. At one point, Joe and his new bride made their way from table to table for obligatory greetings, and, when they got to my table, Joe said something that irritated me. At the distance of forty-five years, I can no longer remember what he said or why I got out of sorts. In any case, I snapped back, rather loudly and nastily. Whether it was my immaturity or something darker that caused my outburst, I don't know. Once Joe and his bride moved away from the table, however, I quickly forgot the incident.

A few weeks later, Joe and Martha invited the entire family to their new home for lunch. "Would you like to see our wedding film?" Joe asked. I'd been unaware of the photographer's presence but joined in the general chorus of "Yes, of course!" Joe threaded the 8 mm film onto the projector, dimmed the lights, and started the movie: Joe and Martha, each getting ready for the wedding; the incomprehensible liturgy; and finally the reception. The camera swept around the room and then followed Joe and Martha as they made their way from table to table. "All right, everyone," Joe announced. "This is the part where Ed yells at me!" As he said that, the incident popped back into my mind. To my horror, it was all there—Joe leaning toward me and saying something into my ear, and my immediate and angry response. It was, of course, a silent film; but the look on my face was unmistakable. I felt humiliated.

For the next several years, every time the family gathered, Joe and Martha would drag out their wedding film. At each showing, he'd make the same announcement: "This is the part where Ed yells at me!" I came to dread family gatherings. They became a source of shame, guilt, and profound embarrassment.

Fast-forward several decades. Joe and Martha and I lost track of one another, but eventually (as often happens in families as people age), we reconnected for a reunion. After dinner, Joe said, "Guess what? Martha and I had our wedding film turned into a video tape. Would you all like to see it?" My heart sank. The incident came storming back into my mind. Everyone else in the room—whether out of mere politeness or with genuine interest, I'll never know—said, "Sure, show the tape!" Before I had a chance to find a way out of the room, I found myself swept back to Joe and Martha's wedding in the early 1960s. There it was: the preparations, the liturgy (no longer incomprehensible; by this time I'd been a priest for almost a quarter century), the reception. Long-dead relatives appeared on the screen as I remembered them from childhood—my grandmother, uncles and aunts, my father. Then the camera began to follow young Joe and Martha around the reception hall, as they once more moved from table to table. "Oh dear God, not *again*," I prayed. Joe and Martha approached my table. The blood pounded in my ears in sync with my rising heart rate. Newlywed Joe leaned toward the fifteen-year-old Ed Little, and I braced myself for the inevitable announcement, my whole body tense—and the scene ended. Joe and Martha walked to the next table. The incident had been edited out, as though it had never happened. The slate had been wiped clean—at Joe's initiative, not mine—and I felt restored, renewed, and whole. A relationship was healed, beyond my deserving.

How do we find the confidence to believe that we have been restored, renewed, made whole? That our relationship with the Father has been healed?

St. Paul begins this section with a contrast. Remember that he has just finished mocking "those who mutilate the flesh" (3:2), a reference to people who advocate circumcision for Gentile Christian converts. He goes on to describe one side of the contrast: "For it is we who are the circumcision, who worship in the Spirit of God and boast in Christ Jesus and have no confidence in the flesh—even though I, too, have reason for confidence in the flesh" (3:3–4a). This is an ongoing theme in Paul's letters. When he writes to the Christians in Rome, for example, he tells them that "real circumcision is a matter of the heart—it is spiritual and not literal" (Romans 2:29). And in his Letter to the Colossians, he draws a parallel between circumcision and Christian baptism, implying that the latter is "spiritual circumcision" (Colossians 2:11–12). The point here is that Paul strongly urges his friends in Philippi to realize that what marks them as believers, what includes them in a covenant relationship with God, is not the outward observance of the ceremonial regulations of the Torah. No, it's a matter of a transformed heart. Physical marks are irrelevant.

By contrast, Paul describes what "confidence in the flesh" looks like, and he does so with reference to his own pre-Christian experience. He ticks off an impressive list of spiritual credentials. "If anyone else has reason for confidence in the flesh, I have more: circumcised on the eighth day, a member of the people of Israel, of the tribe of Benjamin, a Hebrew born of Hebrews; as to the law, a Pharisee; as to zeal, a persecutor of the church; as to righteousness under the law, blameless" (3:4b–6). His religious observance was impeccable, his culture decidedly Jewish ("Hebrew born of Hebrews" refers to the fact that he grew up in an Aramaic-speaking home, despite its location in Tarsus, in what we'd now call southern Turkey), his genealogy flawlessly pure, his zeal so passionate that he'd taken the lead in persecuting the church. Paul doesn't exaggerate the deep commitment he'd made to Jewish life, nor his willingness to invest himself without reservation in hunting down his perceived enemies. He was the real thing, a true believer.

The word "flesh," incidentally, means more than simply the stuff of which we're made, skin and bone and muscle. The Greek word—*sarx*—is sometimes a neutral term (as in, "the Word became flesh [*sarx*] and lived among us," John 1:14, emphasizing the fact that the Son took on the full range of human nature). Often, however, the word carries a negative implication and refers to human nature in its unredeemed state. Thus, in Galatians 5:19, Paul talks about "the works of the flesh" and goes on to list a range of sinful actions and attitudes, some physical (fornication, impurity, licentiousness, idolatry, sorcery, drunkenness, carousing), many intangible (enmities, strife, jealousy, anger, quarrels, dissensions, factions). *Sarx* usually describes humanity in its rebellious state, still saying no to God—and that no manifests itself in a host of activities and attitudes, some obvious, some a matter of inner darkness, invisible but equally destructive. Thus, when Paul talks about his earlier "confidence in the flesh" and follows with his spiritual credentials as a committed Jew, he means that even his religious zeal was unredeemed. It was outwardly pious; but deep inside, where no one but God could see, something was desperately wrong. With that, he turns our attention to what God has done to make things right. Paul was restored, renewed, made whole. His relationship with the Father was healed. The agent of his restoration was the Lord Jesus Christ.

> Yet whatever gains I had, these I have come to regard as loss because of Christ. More than that, I regard everything as loss because of the surpassing value of knowing Christ Jesus my Lord. For his sake, I have suffered the loss of all things, and I regard them as rubbish, in order that I may gain Christ and be found in him, not having a righteousness of my own that comes from the law, but one that comes through faith in Christ, the righteousness from God based on faith. I want to know Christ and the power of his resurrection and the sharing of his sufferings by becoming like him in his death, if somehow I may attain the resurrection from the dead. (3:7–11)

Paul uses vivid language to explain the underlying spiritual realities. His former life, he says, is now "loss"; in fact, it's "rubbish" (the Greek word is *skybala*, a strong and intentionally unpleasant term whose possible permutations of meaning I won't delineate). Paul is telling the story of his conversion—not the specific events in all of their drama, his perse-cution of the church, Jesus' confrontation on the road to Damascus, and Paul's healing and baptism at the hands of Ananias (Acts 9:1–19), but rather the inner dynamic. Here's what was going on, he implies, as my life was shattered and rebuilt. Throughout the Pauline corpus (the body of correspondence bearing his name), Paul returns again and again to this theme. He never tires of telling the story—sometimes simply by brief allusion—of how Jesus rescued him.

Paul goes on to describe three gifts that God has given him, gifts that changed his heart and his life forever.

The first gift is *knowing Jesus* (3:8). When Paul speaks of "the sur-passing value of knowing Christ Jesus my Lord," he's not pointing solely to the facts of Jesus' life and death and resurrection (though these are included). Instead, he's referring to a relationship. The King has sum-moned him, and Paul has received by faith everything that God has accomplished in the faithfulness of Jesus. When Paul talks about Jesus, he's describing not a distant historical character, admired but long dead, but instead a Lord whom he encounters in daily experience. There's a kind of breathlessness in these sentences, as Paul in awe contemplates the wonder of his conversion. The God of the Universe, enthroned above the heavens, has taken notice of him and invited him into a rela-tionship with his Son.

It was this very insight that helped lead me to Christ. As a college sophomore, somewhere in mid journey from atheism to agnosticism to theism to Christianity, I took an astronomy survey course. At one point, the professor used a visual image to try to give his class a picture of the vastness of the cosmos. Imagine, he said, that the earth's orbit around the sun were reduced to the size the head of a pin. If that hap-pened, he went on, our galaxy—the Milky Way, our collection of 100 billion suns—would be the size of the continent of North America. And remember, he added, that there are hundreds of billions of galaxies. Perhaps for some people that visual image would be faith-shattering. If the universe is so big, even if there is a God, how could he ever notice me? How could he be *personal?* Carl Sagan in his famous PBS series *Cosmos* drew that conclusion and encouraged his audience to join him in disbelief: "The cosmos is all there is, all there ever was, and all there ever will be."[1] The image had the opposite effect on me. I found myself overwhelmed by the notion that the God who had created galaxies and clusters of galaxies, the God whose creative variety extended from subatomic particles to unfathomable immensity, knows me and loves me and invites me into a relationship with him. Later, as the journey continued, I took the next step and recognized that God-among-us, the Word Made Flesh, is the sign of this miraculous invitation.

The second gift is *knowing the power of Christ's resurrection* (3:10). We've encountered the theme of power before (2:13). Here, Paul connects it specifically to the resurrection of Jesus. We can do extraordinary things, he implies, because Jesus is risen from the dead. God unleashes that power in us. Paul speaks of this gift more fully in his Letter to the Ephesians, as he prays for his friends in that coastal city in western Asia. I pray, he says, that "you may know what is the hope to which he has called you, what are the riches of his glorious inheritance among the saints, and what is the immeasurable greatness of his power for us who believe, according to the working of his great power. God put this power to work in Christ when he raised him from the dead and seated him at his right hand in the heavenly places" (Ephesians 1:18–20). The explosive and unimaginable energy that reversed death itself has been unleashed on our behalf.

Paul includes in this resurrection gift a brief reference to our own share in Christ's conquest of death (more about that in Chapter 10). "I want to know Christ and the power of his resurrection and the sharing of his sufferings by becoming like him in his death, if somehow I may attain the resurrection from the dead" (3:10–11). The "somehow" here doesn't denote uncertainty (as though Paul were worried about his eternal destiny; he makes it clear in 1:23 that he has no doubts on that score). Instead, he's not attempting to describe the process by which we will be raised. His focus is on the fact of resurrection rather than the details. The point he's making is that he and all Christians not only share in the power of Christ's resurrection now. There's more: that share

---

1. Western Washington University Planetraium, "Cosmic Quotations," http://www .wwu.edu/depts/skywise/cosmo.html.

is a kind of foretaste of eternity, when we will be wondrously raised and will gaze forever into the face of Jesus.

Finally, Paul reminds his friends in Philippi of a third gift—*sharing in Christ's sufferings* (3:10, interestingly, listed *after* "the power of his resurrection"). In Chapter 3, we saw that Paul reminds the Philippians that their sufferings and his are one. But now Paul takes this a step further. Their sufferings and his and ours are Christ's. When we suffer, we are (I'll add my own "somehow") united to Jesus on the cross. That happens on two levels. We can suffer for the sake of the gospel, in major or in minor ways. We may find ourselves out of sync with our families or our culture or even our church. Jesus may call us to risk our lives—or our reputations. He may ask us to place ourselves in harm's way—or, simply, to care for those whose very pain rips our heart asunder. But we can also take the ordinary sufferings that come to us in the course of our lives and offer them up to Jesus. The way of the cross may mean the hidden bearing of pain and seeing in that pain the suffering of our Lord himself. Ron taught me that lesson most powerfully.

It was at the end of a Sunday visitation. The Eucharist was done, the potluck's largesse consumed, the question-and-answer session completed; and the rector invited me to accompany him on a shut-in call. I gladly agreed. On the way to Ron's house, Father Tom told me the tragic story. Ron had been a firefighter, and during what was supposed to be a routine and fairly limited house fire, a floor had collapsed under him. Ron tumbled through the ceiling into the living room and never walked again. His spinal cord was shattered, the damage high enough that he was left paralyzed from the neck down. For several years he had laid at home, cared for by shifts of family and nurses, visited weekly by his priest for Communion. When we arrived at Ron's house, I saw evidence of his former life: pictures of Ron in his firefighter's uniform, photos of Ron and his wife and children on family vacations, a snapshot of Ron playing basketball, caught in midair jamming the ball into the hoop in a jump shot. Then, I was ushered into Ron's room, what had once been the downstairs study, a large picture window looking out onto the back lawn and, beyond, a stand of trees. Ron lay on a hospital bed, thinner than he appeared in any of the photos and, of course, completely immobilized, his hands outside the covers, utterly still.

We chatted for a while and then shared the Eucharist together. Ron wondered how heavy my pectoral cross is (that's the large, usually gold, cross that bishops traditionally wear); so I lifted up his hand in mine and placed the cross on his palm. Finally, I asked Ron, "How do you spend your days?" He paused for a long time. "The afternoons especially are endless," he said. "Sometimes I just look out the window and watch the trees as they change from season to season. But that's pretty slow, isn't it? Sometimes I watch television—as long as someone turns it on and switches it to a channel I'm interested in—but after a while even Oprah gets old. Mostly I look at Jesus on the cross." I followed his eyes to a crucifix on the wall next to the sliding glass door. There was Jesus, graphically depicted, his tortured body still, a gash in his side, his arms at a forty-five-degree angle as he stretched forward in death. "Mostly I look at Jesus on the cross." He didn't need to say any more. Ron knew more about the suffering of Jesus than I. He saw in the suffering of Jesus a mirror of his own and had somehow been empowered to offer his suffering to his crucified Lord. His faith challenged mine.

St. Paul's journey—from confidence in the flesh to confidence in Jesus—is both a model and an encouragement. Jesus restored him, renewed him, made him whole, and healed his relationship with the Father. Jesus makes that same gift available to us. And, as we will see in the next chapter, the process is far from complete. Our Lord has much in store for Paul and for us.

QUESTIONS FOR REFLECTION

1. Paul describes his former life as embodying "confidence in the flesh." What is your equivalent? What do you rely on?

2. How have you come to know Jesus? When did his name become more than just a word to you? How did he move from being a historical figure to a living and contemporary Lord?

3. How have you experienced the power of the resurrection in your life?

4. In what ways have you been able to see in your own sufferings the sufferings of Jesus himself?

CHAPTER 9

Growing in Jesus

Philippians 3:12–16

*W*hat shall we do with the Ring? That's the question facing a great Council gathered at Rivendell, midway through the first volume of J. R. R. Tolkien's *The Lord of the Rings*. The Ring, granting enormous power to the one who wears it, has fallen (not quite by accident) into the care of the hobbit Bilbo Baggins and then his nephew Frodo. Whoever wears the Ring will ultimately be destroyed, since the Ring had been fashioned by the evil Sauron. Gathered at the elf Elrond's home at Rivendell are representatives of many races: Gimli the dwarf, two human beings (Boromir and Aragorn), the elf Legolas from Lothlorien, the wizard Gandalf the Grey, and the humble hobbits Frodo and Bilbo, short, shoeless, and barely marked among the great and mighty. What shall we do with the Ring? There is only one way to destroy it: to cast it into the volcanic fires of Mount Doom, in the midst of Sauron's evil empire. Does anyone have the courage to undertake such a perilous—and probably futile—journey?

The great and mighty sit in silence. No one dares look another in the eye. Time passes with agonizing slowness. Finally, from the midst of the silence, Frodo speaks, his voice trembling: "'I will take the Ring,' he said, 'though I do not know the way.'"[1] Frodo is the least qualified,

---

1. J. R. R. Tolkien, *The Lord of the Rings: The Fellowship of the Ring* (1955; New York: Ballantine Books, 1973), 324.

the most untrained, and utterly unsuited for such a task. Hobbits live in the Shire, far from the centers of power in Middle Earth. They are a simple people, unsophisticated and (in outward appearance) a little foolish. At the Council of Elrond, Frodo sits unnoticed as the mighty debate the future of the world. Yet it is Frodo who assumes the task and who, in the end, summons both the courage and the energy to invade the heartland of Sauron.

I have often seen in the role of Frodo an icon of Christian discipleship. We too are unqualified, untrained, and unsuited for the task of winning the world for Jesus Christ. Jesus could manifestly do better in selecting disciples. St. Paul himself would, I think, agree with that assessment, as he looks at his own experience as a follower of Jesus.

One might conclude, incorrectly I believe, that Paul had achieved a certain level of Christian perfection. As he describes his conversion in Philippians 3:7–11, the words seem almost triumphalistic. He knows Jesus, his life is conformed to Jesus' death, and he's experiencing the power of the resurrection. This is heady stuff indeed, and one might be tempted to ascribe to Paul the doctrine of "entire sanctification" that became a hallmark of the Holiness Movement of the nineteenth century. And so, lest his friends in Philippi draw the wrong conclusion, Paul goes on to offer a "truth in advertising" disclaimer. He makes it clear that he is *far* from perfection; that he is, spiritually speaking, still a child or at best an adolescent; that his growth and development is an ongoing and significantly incomplete process. "Not that I have already obtained this, or have already reached the goal" (3:12a), Paul says as he begins this section. The phrase "reached the goal" in the New Revised Standard Version of the Bible is something of a paraphrase, putting it in parallel with verse 14. But the word in verse 12 is actually *teteleiomai*, which means literally "have been perfected." (Many other translations—for instance, the New International Version, the Revised English Bible, and the Revised Standard Version—take a more literal approach in rendering *teteleiomai*.) Some commentators see in this verb a veiled reference to ancient mystery cults, secret societies that claimed one could achieve perfection by learning special "knowledge" known only to the initiated. These mystery cults were the New Age of their day. If you know the right things, you've been perfected. Paul, by contrast, says that he *hasn't* been perfected. Christianity is no mystery cult, and knowing Jesus is far more profound than acquiring secret knowledge that perfects the initiated.

Whether Paul refers to ancient mystery cults is debatable; but Paul's point is clear. Jesus has much to accomplish in him. Paul is describing a holy dissatisfaction, a perpetual discontentment with his own discipleship. His understanding of the faith and his living out of the gospel's demands must still be honed. "But I press on," Paul continues, "because Christ Jesus has made me his own" (3:12b). Despite his imperfection, Paul never forgets his conversion. He can be honest about his spiritual shortcomings because he knows that Jesus has already taken the first step, has grasped him supernaturally. The very thing that Jesus has done in his life—throwing him to the ground on the road to Damascus, transforming his life forever—gives Paul permission to acknowledge the unformed nature of his life in Christ.

In 1973, my wife, Sylvia, and I moved to Anaheim, California, where I began my second curacy as assistant rector of St. Michael's Church. It happened that the Sunday of my arrival coincided with the parish's one-hundredth anniversary celebration. A century earlier, Susan LaFaucherie and a hardy band of Episcopalians had founded St. Michael's in what was then the wilderness of Orange County. And so, in the spring of 1973, dignitaries and former parishioners from all around the country converged in Anaheim for the centennial celebration, among them the Rt. Rev. Robert Gooden, retired bishop suffragan of the Diocese of Los Angeles. Because I was the new curate, completely unaware of St. Michael's liturgical customs, I was assigned the task of serving as Bishop Gooden's chaplain (essentially, getting him into the church, properly seated, and then out of the church and over to the parish hall for the reception). In that capacity, the centennial organizers reasoned, I could do the least harm. My assignment turned out to be a great gift.

Bishop Gooden was ninety-eight years old at the time of St. Michael's centennial. (He died three years later at the age of 101.) Still surprisingly spry, his main disability was dimming eyesight. His hearing and, above all, his mind remained sharp. I will never forget our conversation as we prepared for the opening procession. He told me that his greatest disappointment as he'd gotten older was that he could no longer read the Old Testament lesson in Morning and Evening Prayer in the original Hebrew. Oh, he could still read the New Testament lesson in Greek; but Hebrew presented a more difficult challenge for his eyes. In Hebrew, the vowel signs look like small hen scratches underneath the larger consonants. Bishop Gooden's eyesight had declined to the point that he couldn't make out the vowels; and so, much to his sorrow, he'd been reduced to reading the Old Testament lesson in English. I remember my awe as I contemplated this ancient and godly man who still yearned to deepen his faith. At the age of ninety-eight, he hadn't arrived. He was, like Paul himself, far from perfection—and he knew it. Many years later, I find myself returning again and again to Bishop Gooden's holy dissatisfaction and yearning to follow his example.

"Beloved," Paul tells his friends in Philippi, "I do not consider that I have made it my own; but this one thing I do: forgetting what lies behind and straining forward to what lies ahead, I press on toward the goal for the prize of the heavenly call of God in Christ Jesus" (3:13–14). Paul is using the language of an athletic contest, a common New Testament analogy. In his First Letter to the Corinthians, for example, Paul is even more expansive: "Do you not know that in a race the runners all compete, but only one receives the prize? Run in such a way that you may win it. Athletes exercise self-control in all things; they do it to receive a perishable wreath; but we an imperishable one. So I do not run aimlessly, nor do I box as though beating the air; but I punish my body and enslave it, so that after proclaiming to others I myself should not be disqualified" (1 Corinthians 9:24–27). In the ancient world, athletic contests were major public events. Paul's readers would be familiar both with the intensity with which athletes compete and with the prize they were competing for—a laurel wreath placed on the winner's head as a crown, the equivalent of an Olympic gold medal. And so Paul and other New Testament writers use this image frequently as a picture of Christian discipleship (see also 1 Timothy 6:12; 2 Timothy 4:7–8; Hebrews 12:1). Like athletes, Christians work hard and remain focused on a goal. Like athletes, Christians exert enormous energy "for the prize of the heavenly call" (3:14). Like athletes, Christians grow.

Paul is describing a journey, albeit an inner one. He's picking up on a theme that permeates the Bible. The scriptures regularly portray characters on the move; and the very act of going from one place to another reveals the heart of God. Abraham travels from Ur of the Chaldeans to Haran to the Promised Land to Egypt and back to the Promised Land. Jacob makes a tortured journey from Beer-sheba to Haran and back again, with significant stops at Bethel and Peniel. The Israelites wander in the desert for forty years, guided by a pillar of cloud and a pillar of fire. The Jews travel as exiles from Jerusalem to Babylon and return years later when Cyrus the Persian issues his edict. Jesus and the Twelve journey throughout Galilee and, after three years, turn their faces to Jerusalem. The Apostle Paul himself undertakes three missionary journeys and finally, in chains, travels to Rome. Indeed, much of the world's greatest literature centers on the theme of journey: the *Odyssey* of Homer, the *Aeneid* of Virgil, Chaucer's *Canterbury Tales*, Dante's *Divine Comedy*, and—in our own era—*The Lord of the Rings*. What all of these journeys, biblical and otherwise, have in common is transformation. The travelers change. Something happens inside them. When the journey is done, they are no longer the same.

Neither is Paul. He is partway through a journey. It began on the road to Damascus, with profound roots in his earlier devotion to Judaism. It will end (or better, will continue in a transfigured way) in the beatific vision. Meanwhile, Paul says that he will do three things.

First, "I press on" (3:14a). He's intentional about growth. After all, growth doesn't happen automatically. It involves hard work and a daily decision, and Paul is well aware that he must commit time and energy to the task. That principle is essential for us, too. If we want our relationship with God in Christ to deepen, we must invest ourselves. The traditional disciplines of the spiritual life—prayer, reading, and reflecting on scripture, silence, and immersion in Christian community—all require that we *do* something, that we "press on." Like Paul, we're all in the middle of a process, one that began when we came to Christ in baptism and in conscious commitment, one that ends (and continues) when we see Jesus face-to-face in heaven. Meanwhile, Jesus invites us to be "giving up our selves to [God's] service."[2] The Episcopal Church's

2. *Book of Common Prayer* (New York: Oxford University Press, 1979), 101.

baptismal liturgy captures something of this journey-begun or journey-far-from-finished dynamic. Immediately after the candidates have been baptized, the priest or bishop prays, "Heavenly Father, we thank you that by water and the Holy Spirit you have bestowed upon these your servants the forgiveness of sin, and have raised them to the new life of grace. Sustain them, O Lord, in your Holy Spirit. Given them an inquiring and discerning heart, the courage to will and to persevere, a spirit to know and to love you, and the gift of joy and wonder in all your works. *Amen.*"[3]

The prayer recognizes that something has already happened, that God has acted in a powerful and decisive way in the newly baptized person's life, offering the gifts of forgiveness and new life. But the prayer goes on to acknowledge an important reality: there's more to come. Baptism is a beginning, and now the new Christian must undertake a journey of discovery, a journey filled with surprises, unexpected twists and turns, and, ultimately, joy and wonder.

Second, Paul presses on "toward the goal of the prize of the heavenly call of God in Christ Jesus" (3:14b). The journey isn't aimless for Paul or for us. We're going somewhere. (We will look at this more in-depth in the next chapter.) Paul is clear about the goal. It isn't the laurel wreath of Greek athletic contests but a prize infinitely more precious. The prize, above all, centers on Jesus. He is not talking about a vague "spirituality"—learning more about yourself, about life, about what makes the universe tick—but about getting to know Jesus better and about following him more faithfully. For Christians, spirituality can never be separated from Jesus. The journey is always Christ-ward, or it is not a Christian journey at all. Even if the next steps remain clouded in fog, we know that, when the fog lifts, we will see Jesus himself.

> I know not where the road will lead
> I follow day by day,
> Ort where it end: I only know
> I walk the King's highway.[4]

---

3. Ibid., 101.
4. *The Hymnal 1982* (New York: Church Hymnal Corporation, 1985), Hymn 647.

Finally, Paul reminds his friends in Philippi that they are in this for the long haul. "Only let us hold fast to what we have attained" (3:16). "Hold fast" actually translates a Greek verb (*stoichein*) that means "to walk," a common way that the New Testament speaks of living. "Live in love, as Christ loved us" (Ephesians 5:2), Paul tells the Christian community in Ephesus; and again the verb, literally rendered, is "walk." The journey won't be done in a day or a week or a year or a lifetime. Often, the most important insights come at the end of a long, arduous, and time-consuming journey, when we least expect them. Persistence is a necessary virtue in the business of discipleship.

So it was that Bill's eyes were opened—late in life, but not too late. Bill was a member of my parish in Bakersfield, California; he joined the congregation about the time that I arrived. He was, however, a long-time Christian from another denomination and quite serious about his faith. Every Sunday, after the 8:00 a.m. Eucharist (he and his wife, Marion, always sat in the front row), he'd attend a between-services Bible study. His questions were perceptive, often probing, and never frivolous. Since the class worked its way sequentially through books of the Bible, he would read passages in advance and was well-prepared for the discussion. He had a wonderful curiosity about the scriptures, and no detail—about history, literary form, or archeology—escaped his attention. And so, one morning, we were working our way verse by verse through the Gospel according to St. John. We'd arrived at the fourteenth chapter, toward the beginning of the long speech that Jesus gave at the Last Supper. Thomas asks his famous question ("Lord, we do not know where you are going. How can we know the way?"), and Jesus gives his equally famous answer ("I am the way, and the truth, and the life. No one comes to the Father except through me"). The class considered the implications of the exclusive claim that Jesus makes for himself (John 14:5–6), and then we turned our attention to another challenge, this one from Philip. "Lord, show us the Father, and we will be satisfied." Jesus replies, "Have I been with you all this time, Philip, and you still do not know me? Whoever has seen me has seen the Father" (John 14:8–9).

At that point I restated the teaching found in John's Gospel about the incarnation, a teaching that has its origin in the prologue and specifically in John 1:14. All of this, I thought, was basically a review. Jesus not only reveals the Father; he is, in an absolutely unique way, the revelation of God, God scaled down (so to speak) in the flesh-and-blood Jesus. When you look at Jesus—as fully human as you or I—you're looking at God himself in human form. It took the church several centuries to work out what this means and to find vocabulary to describe it; but the doctrine itself has its roots embedded deeply in the New Testament, from the Gospels to the Epistles to the book of Revelation. I didn't think I was saying anything particularly startling. But suddenly, Bill looked up and said, quite loudly, "Wait a minute!" He had everybody's attention. "Father Ed, are you saying that Jesus is *God*?" I said, "Yes, I am." "I didn't know that," Bill said. "Why didn't anybody tell me this before?" At that moment, after decades of faithful Bible reading, something profound happened. For the very first time, Bill came to understand a central teaching of the Christian faith. He'd heard the teaching over and over. One can hardly avoid it at Christmas time; the Feast of the Nativity, after all, is far more than sentimental baby worship, and carol after carol emphasizes the point (look at the text of "O Come, All Ye Faithful," for example). Somehow, though, this essential biblical truth hadn't touched Bill's heart and mind. I'll never know why it took so long. In the end, it doesn't really matter. In God's good time and through Bill's faithful persistence, he made the connection.

Paul offers something of a disclaimer near the end of this section. "Let those of us then who are mature be of the same mind; and if you think differently about anything, this too God will reveal to you" (3:15). This is a word of humility on Paul's part. He recognizes that, as is always the case when people discuss matters touching the Christian faith, there will be disputed points. Don't let them sidetrack you or become the cause of division, he says. Remember that, in the end, God will make everything clear. In the meantime, he tells his friends in Philippi, keep your focus where it ought to be—your eye on "the prize of the heavenly call of God in Christ Jesus" (3:14).

QUESTIONS FOR REFLECTION

1. What spiritual disciplines have been most helpful in assisting you to grow as a Christian?

2. How do you find yourself resisting growth? What gets in the way and makes it difficult for you to invest yourself in spiritual disciplines?

3. What are the significant markers in your spiritual journey? When have the "turning points" occurred? What facilitated them?

4. Who in your life has modeled a pattern of spiritual growth? How have they encouraged and challenged you?

CHAPTER 10

Dual Citizenship

Philippians 3:17–21

"What do we do now?" These are the famous closing words of the political film *The Candidate*. Young Bill McKay (a Kennedyesque figure played by Robert Redford) has been running for a seat in the U.S. Senate. For months, he has invested himself completely in the electoral process. He's given speech after speech after speech, to the point that he sometimes sounds like an automaton. (He's also made compromise after compromise after compromise, setting aside his ideals in order to win votes; but that's another story.) Now, finally, he's done it. Against all odds, he's defeated the veteran Senator Crocker Jarmon, a clever and canny political warrior. At the victory party, he sits in the midst of his cheering supporters, dazed, unable to process the wonderful (or terrible) thing that's happened to him. He has beaten the odds, conquered the unconquerable, and risen into the stratosphere of political power and influence. Still in his thirties, Bill McKay has achieved greatness. Finally, he looks up, his face confused, his gaze faraway, and says to his campaign manager: "What do we do now?"

Indeed, what do *we* do now? Perhaps, like Bill McKay, we too are dazed. Paul has been exhorting his Philippian friends—and us—to faithfulness. On one level, we understand what he means, and we've started to do it. We're running the race. Jesus invites us to invest ourselves completely in the process of discipleship. And so, as consciously as we could, we have turned away from sin and from whatever separates us from God and others. We've committed our lives to Jesus Christ and embarked on a journey of spiritual growth. We can see, as we look back at our experience, glimmers of success. At least occasionally we've managed to yield ourselves to the Lord. But what do we do now? What's next? Surprisingly, before turning to some very practical directions in Philippians 4, St. Paul sets his sights on the distant future, on eternity itself. We discover the next step by looking into the face of Jesus in heaven and pondering our eternal destiny.

Philippians 3 tells the story in three tenses. First, Paul reminds us of the past (Philippians 3:7–11). He looks back at his own conversion and the events that preceded it, and in so doing asks us to consider our own journey to faith. Then there's the present (3:12–16) and Paul's contention that the journey is ongoing, a process rather than a single event. Finally, Paul turns to the future, the Philippians' and ours (3:17–21), and the promise that we have a home with Jesus that will outlast even the physical universe when, billions of years from now, entropy brings eternal darkness and silence. Paul begins the final section of the chapter with a word of encouragement and a word of warning.

The word of encouragement has to do with his own role in the task of disciple-making. "Brothers and sisters," he says, "join in imitating me, and observe those who live according to the example you have in us" (3:17). At first glance, this sounds rather self-congratulatory. But remember that when Paul wrote to his friends in Philippi, what we call the New Testament didn't exist. Stories about Jesus were circulating in oral form, but the four Gospels were still unwritten. Paul's letters had not been recognized as having canonical status (in other words, they were simply letters and not—yet!—holy scripture; it was for later generations to discern their sacred character). The way that a Christian learned to live the Christian life was primarily to watch other Christians. As I write these words, faces pass before my mind's eye: a college roommate who first (oh so gently) shared the good news with me, a long-dead colleague whose gift of encouragement changed my life and redirected my ministry, parishioners whose vibrant faith challenged me when I was at my "highest and driest," my beloved wife, friends in this country and around the world, a whole host of God's people who have embodied the Christian faith in costly and powerful ways—the "cloud of witnesses" (Hebrews 12:1) whom I mentioned at the end of Chapter 1. Paul quite rightly urges his Philippian friends to take note of people whose lives are a kind of "living gospel" and to follow their example.

A word of warning, however, takes Paul into more difficult territory. "For many live as enemies of the cross of Christ," he says. "I have often told you of them, and now I tell you even with tears. Their end is destruction; their god is the belly; and their glory is in their shame; their minds are set on earthly things" (3:18–19). No one knows precisely who these people were. Some commentators understand the phrase "their god is the belly" as a comic reference to those who continued to follow the kosher food regulations of the Torah. (It is indeed one of Paul's funnier lines!) Perhaps, they argue, Paul sees people who are obsessed with food as unintentionally deifying their gastrointestinal system. That may be. Other scholars, by contrast, think that the opponents Paul mentions here were actually "antinomians," people who have convinced themselves that, since they belong to Jesus, no moral constraints limit their behavior. They're free to do anything they want, since the body isn't important anyway. And so they turn their natural appetites into little "gods" and relapse almost unconsciously into the paganism that they think they've renounced.

In any case, there's something bogus about these people. I find myself thinking about the spam that clutters my inbox with every download. Quite regularly, for example, I receive e-mail offering me a "replica Rolex" for a ridiculously low price. In the picture on my computer screen, the watch looks like a Rolex. I imagine that on my wrist it would feel like a Rolex. It might even fool my friends. The trouble is, it isn't a Rolex. It's a cheap imitation that bears a remarkable resemblance to a real Rolex—without possessing the inner reality. And that's the phenomenon that Paul is urging his friends in Philippi to avoid. It's possible, he says, for someone to bear all the outward marks of Christian discipleship but to be less than the genuine article: baptized, yes, confirmed, even ordained (this is a terrifying thought), but a heart far from God (see Jesus' words in Mark 7:6), deep in rebellion. This is a warning, incidentally, that's not only about *them*, about false disciples of the first century.

103

It's also about us. Take heed, Paul implies, that our actions match our outward profession of faith. Don't enshrine as gods what cannot save.

Then Paul turns his attention to the future. He's struggling for words to describe something well beyond our experience; and so he uses an analogy that his Philippians friends will understand. "But our citizenship is in heaven, and it is from there that we are expecting a Savior, the Lord Jesus Christ. He will transform the body of our humiliation that it may be conformed to the body of his glory, by the power that also enables him to make all things subject to himself" (3:20–21). In these dense but powerful phrases centering on our "citizenship . . . in heaven," Paul talks about who we are and what Jesus is doing in our lives.

Let's begin with who we are. Citizenship was a major issue in the city of Philippi. As citizens of a Roman colony, Philippians were also accorded the privilege of Roman citizenship, no small matter. It's difficult for us—I write as an American citizen and realize that the "us" may not include all readers of this book—fully to grasp the implications of citizenship in the Empire. In the United States, citizenship is conferred by birth or naturalization, the first coming automatically, the second requiring a difficult, time-consuming, but ultimately manageable procedure. My son was adopted from Korea, and so I've seen naturalization at close range. Greg was just five-months old when he came to the United States, and, after a complex and sometimes frustrating bureaucratic process, he became a citizen at the age of five. I remember standing with him in the Ahmanson Center in Los Angeles, surrounded by thousands of other immigrants, as a judge administered the oath of citizenship. The feeling of joy in the room was quite palpable: joy, I imagine, that combined gratitude for the fact of citizenship and relief that the arduous process was done!

In the Roman Empire, on the other hand, citizenship was far from automatic and far from easily obtained. A small percentage of the population was born as citizens, others purchased it, and some—like the citizens of Philippi—acquired it through military service. Becoming a Roman citizen involved a process far more complicated and far less certain than anything devised by the Immigration and Naturalization Service. It's no surprise that most of the Empire's residents didn't benefit from this privilege.

And privilege it was. Roman citizens, for example, enjoyed certain legal protections not guaranteed to others. Citizens couldn't be beaten or tortured by the police before trial, and they had the right to appeal to the emperor when sentenced in a court of law. Paul himself was a Roman citizen, a legal trump card that he used on a number of occasions. In Philippi itself, Paul and Silas were beaten after their arrest (Acts 16:23); the city officials apparently failed to inquire about their status. Following the dramatic events surrounding their night in jail (Acts 16:25–34), the magistrates order their release, and Paul sends back a message: "They have beaten us in public, uncondemned, men who are Roman citizens, and have thrown us into prison; and now are they going to discharge us in secret?" (Acts 16:37). The magistrates, recognizing their legal faux pas, quickly let Paul and Silas go. Later, in Jerusalem, Paul asks a centurion who's about to beat him, "Is it legal for you to flog a Roman citizen who is uncondemned?" (Acts 22:25). In an ensuing dialogue with the tribune (the centurion's superior), the tribune says to Paul, "It cost me a large sum of money to get my citizenship," and Paul replies, "But I was born a citizen" (Acts 22:28–29). Paul relies on this legal protection when, facing the possibility of trial in Jerusalem before a hostile court, he appeals to the Emperor (Acts 25:10–12).

All of this makes Paul's contention particularly startling. "Our citizenship is in heaven" (3:20). To Christians who must have basked in the legal protections and social status conferred by Roman citizenship, Paul asserts that their real homeland is elsewhere. Whatever privileges the Roman Empire has conferred upon you, he implies, pale in comparison to what you receive as a citizen of heaven itself. There's a sense, Paul is telling his friends, in which you have one foot in this world and one in the world to come—a teaching that he alludes to in other passages as well. "Blessed be the God and Father of our Lord Jesus Christ," he says to the Christian community in Ephesus, "who has blessed us in Christ with every spiritual blessing in the heavenly places. . . . [God has] raised us up with [Christ] and seated us with him in the heavenly places in Christ Jesus" (Ephesians 1:3; 2:6). The traditional New Testament reading for Easter Day makes the same point: "So if you have been raised with Christ, seek the things that are above, where Christ is, seated at the right hand of God. Set your minds on things that are above, not on things that are on earth. For you have died, and your life is hidden with Christ in God. When Christ who is your life is revealed, then you also will be revealed with him in glory" (Colossians 3:1–4).

Paul is describing a kind of "dual citizenship." On the one hand, he doesn't hesitate in the face of legal harassment to stand on the privileges of being a citizen of the Roman Empire. On the other, he reminds his friends that heaven isn't simply a destination. It's their home now, and Christians experience glimpses in this life of their eternal destiny.

My religious background is decidedly mixed. My mother was a Lithuanian Jew. Her parents immigrated to the United States early in the twentieth century and passed through Ellis Island; those who stayed behind perished in the Kovno Ghetto during World War II. My father descended from Irish, English and Scottish stock, with denominational origins as varied as Puritan Congregationalist (some of my ancestors helped to hang witches in Salem), Anglican, and Roman Catholic. That accounts, I suppose, for my relentlessly secular upbringing. Despite being baptized as an infant in the Episcopal Church, my parents could never quite settle on any one tradition and eventually chose none. As things have shaken out, I've ended up a Christian and my beloved sister, Jane, a Jew. The Old and New Covenants adhere in a single family.

I will never forget my sister's awed description of her first trip to the Holy Land. She traveled to Israel with a group of Jewish pilgrims, the El Al jet filled with Jews as diverse as liberal Reform, pious Orthodox, and secular nonbelievers. Some travelers ate, drank, and watched movies throughout the long flight, others prayed and davened and prepared themselves spiritually. When the jet landed at Lod Airport in Tel Aviv, however, the atmosphere changed. People began weeping, some uncontrollably. Others cheered and clapped and sang. For Jews, Israel is more than a strip of land with a pleasant Mediterranean climate. In a post-Holocaust world, it is home: a place of safety and belonging. The planeload of pilgrims who landed in Tel Aviv that day discovered the joy—and the tension—of dual citizenship (in this case, not formal, but experiential). Americans all, they belonged here, and they belonged there.

Christians have something important to learn from the Jewish experience, for we too hold dual citizenship. We cannot help being *here*. We are creatures of flesh and blood and spirit, rooted in our own planet, our own culture, the network of family and friends and co-workers and fellow Christians who inhabit our lives and our hearts. At the same time, we are *there*. Heaven too is our home, and we are citizens of eternity, already claimed by the King of kings as his own. That's who we are, and our lives this side of the grave will always be filled with the joy and the tension of dual citizenship.

Then, Paul turns his attention to Jesus—and what he's doing in our lives. Jesus, Paul tells his friends, "will transform the body of our humiliation that it may be conformed to the body of his glory" (3:21). In other words, we will be like him (see 1 John 3:2). Somehow, when we see him face-to-face, we will be clothed with a body as glorious as his, no longer limited by time and space, no longer subject to death and decay. This is a far cry from the "immortality of the soul" found in Greek philosophy, the notion that when we die what survives is the disembodied, immaterial soul that's been trapped during our earthly years in an imperfect and impure body. The New Testament concept is quite different. God will raise us up with Jesus and will give us a new body like Jesus' own resurrected and glorified body. Paul struggles to find words to capture this wonderful promise. He writes the Christian community in Corinth, "What is sown"—the implication is "sown in the ground," that is, buried—"is perishable, what is raised is imperishable. It is sown in dishonor, it is raised in glory. It is sown in weakness, it is raised in power" (1 Corinthians 15:42–43). When we read the accounts of Jesus' resurrection, we catch glimmers of what Paul means. The risen Jesus was recognizably Jesus, the same person whom the disciples had followed in Galilee and who had been crucified on Good Friday. After his resurrection, he could eat and drink, teach and exhort, walk and talk. And yet, at the same time, he was changed, transformed. He could suddenly turn up in a room, despite the fact that the doors were locked (John 20:19). Sometimes his disciples failed to recognize him until "their eyes were opened" (Luke 24:31; see also John 21:16; 21:7). Eventually he ascended to the Father, no longer physically present; yet he promised to be "with you always, to the end of the age" (Matthew 28:20).

All of this, of course, is beyond our experience. We cannot know what it is like to possess a glorified body, because the body we now inhabit is so markedly impermanent. Every day I'm reminded that it won't last. When my ophthalmologist tells me that I need a new prescription because I'm suffering from "presbyopia," I know enough Greek to realize that "presbyopia" simply means "old eyes." Our bodies wear out, and we aren't capable of fully comprehending what it means to be granted a new one. We do know this, however, that citizenship in heaven, both now and in eternity, means looking at Jesus. In this life, our vision is imperfect. We see Jesus in his body, the church, and in the miracle that each Christian represents the risen Christ. "Each individual layman," says *Lumen Gentium*, the Second Vatican Council's decree on the Church, "must stand before the world as a witness to the resurrection and life of the Lord Jesus and as a sign that God lives."[1] We see Jesus in our mind's eye as we pray and reflect on the scriptures. We see Jesus most wondrously in the Blessed Sacrament of his body and blood. But all of this is foretaste, as we prepare for that vision, which is eternal, when the veil is pulled back and we gaze at him forever in heaven.

C. S. Lewis's *The Screwtape Letters* contains a series of epistles from a chief demon in hell to a tempter-in-training on earth. The chief demon, Screwtape, advises his nephew Wormwood, who's at work on his first "case"; Screwtape tries to help Wormwood to find ways to lure his "patient" out of the hands of the Enemy. (The Enemy is Screwtape's title for Jesus.) Wormwood tries device after infernal device, but none of them bear fruit. Neither spiritual pride nor sexual temptation nor various watered-down versions of Christianity make headway in the "patient's" heart and mind. In the end, Wormwood fails and the "patient" dies a committed Christian. Screwtape describes the scene when the veil is suddenly pulled back:

> He saw not only Them [a surrounding army of angels]; he saw Him. This animal, this thing begotten in a bed, could look on Him. What is blinding, suffocating fire to you is now cool light to him, is clarity itself, and wears the form of a Man. You would like, if you could, to interpret the patient's prostration in the Presence, his self-abhorrence and utter knowledge of his sins (yes, Wormwood, a clearer knowledge

1. Walter M. Abbott, SJ, ed., *The Documents of Vatican II* (New York: Guild Press, 1966), 65.

even than yours) on the analogy of your own choking and paralyzing sensation when you encounter the deadly air that breathes from the heart of Heaven. But it's all nonsense. Pains he may still have to encounter, but they *embrace* those pains. They would not barter them for any earthly pleasure. All the delights of sense or heart or intellect with which you could once have tempted him, even the delights of virtue itself, now seem to him in comparison but as the half-nauseous attractions of a raddled harlot would seem to a man who hears that his true beloved whom he has loved all his life and whom he had believed to be dead is alive and even now at his door. He is caught up into that world where pain and pleasure take on transfinite values and where all our arithmetic is dismayed.[2]

Someday we too will gaze at Jesus, "clarity itself, and wear[ing] the form of a Man," as we see the one who "will transform the body of our humiliation that it may be conformed to the body of his glory" (3:21).

QUESTIONS FOR REFLECTION

1. Some of Paul's opponents worship a false god ("their god is the belly"). How are you tempted to substitute something in place of God?

2. Who do you mark as an example of Christian living? Who are the "living gospels" in your life?

3. What are the signposts of your citizenship in heaven? The reminders that you have a permanent home elsewhere?

4. However imperfectly, what are the ways that you see Jesus face-to-face in your daily life?

---

2. C. S. Lewis, *The Screwtape Letters* (1943; New York: Macmillan Company, 1961), 148.

PART IV

The Peace of God

*P*aul begins the fourth chapter of Philippians with another "therefore" reminder. "Therefore, my brothers and sisters, whom I love and long for, my joy and crown, stand firm in the Lord in the Lord in this way, my beloved" (4:1). He's looking back at all that he has just said about confidence in Jesus. You know Jesus, you're growing in Jesus, and you can be certain of your eternal destiny: therefore, stand firm.

But something gets in the way. Apparently, two women in the congregation in Philippi have fallen into significant, perhaps church-dividing, conflict. "I urge Euodia and I urge Syntyche," he says, "to be of the same mind in the Lord. Yes, and I ask you also, my loyal companion, help these women, for they have struggled beside me in the work of the gospel, together with Clement and the rest of my co-workers, whose names are in the book of life" (4:2–3). Paul urges his "loyal companion" (the Greek word here, *Syzygus*, may be a name or a title) to intervene. We don't know the details of the conflict. Was it over some trivial issue or a major one? Was it driven by strong personalities? Had the conflict spiraled out and drawn in the entire congregation? Paul doesn't say. Certainly this isn't a phenomenon limited to Philippi. The New Testament is filled with reports of conflict in the apostolic community, starting with James and John and their mother jockeying for power (Matthew 20:20–28), continuing with the personality-driven division in Corinth (1 Corinthians 1:10–13), and including even the quarrel between Paul himself and his traveling companion Barnabas (Acts 15:36–41). Even the most committed Christians find themselves divided. The conflict in Philippi, certainly, isn't between troublemakers, not at all. These women have "struggled beside" Paul in his ministry.

Yet things have gone terribly and tragically wrong. The conflict threatens to rob the Philippian church of its peace. And so Paul devotes the final section of his letter to his friends in Philippi, not simply to resolving the specific conflict, but to providing some general principles. How can Christians discover "the peace of God, which surpasses all understanding" (Philippians 4:7)? How can peace be restored, in the face of division? What concrete steps do Christians need to take when conflict threatens the church? That is where Paul turns his attention, as he concludes his letter.

Be Gentle

Philippians 4:4–5

I experienced something of a revelation in the summer of 2004. The political season was in full swing, and the two major parties gathered to nominate candidates for president of the United States. Since I'm something of a political junkie, I tuned into the conventions every night to see what surprises might be in the offing. (There were none, of course. National conventions nowadays are carefully scripted from start to finish. Gone is the drama that surrounded the choosing of a presidential nominee. The outcome was determined much earlier, in the primary season.) Night after night, as the conventions dragged on, I found myself disgusted by the rhetoric. Speeches seemed to contain two essential elements: clever sound bites (speechwriters apparently look for witty turns of phrase that are memorable yet content-free) and nasty personal attacks on the character and motives of the opposing party's nominee. In disgust, I turned one evening to a cable station that was rebroadcasting presidential acceptance speeches going all the way back to Franklin D. Roosevelt's in 1932. That first night, I stumbled onto the 1956 speeches of President Dwight D. Eisenhower and his opponent, Governor Adlai Stevenson, and watched in fascination. Two things surprised me. First, the speeches contained ideas. Both nominees talked about specific proposals and tried to articulate an overarching political philosophy. Second, the speeches carefully avoid personal attack. In fact, neither nominee mentioned his opponent by name. Politics is never a gentle occupation. In the end, politicians are trying to outmaneuver and defeat their opponents. Yet, after listening to those speeches from 1956, I couldn't help but be saddened by the change in tone and rhetoric that has come in the intervening decades. We live in a toxic era.

Things are no better in the church and, particularly, in the dangerous arena known as cyberspace. I remember, for example, the first time I got "flamed." (That's an Internet term referring to a multipronged e-mail attack.) I was taking part in an online "list" (another Internet term; it's a kind of digital bulletin board in which people post ideas and respond to the ideas of others), and the discussion had turned to the difficult and divisive topic of same-sex unions. Should the church provide a liturgical form to bless these relationships? Several people posted notes in which they argued in favor of such a provision. Although I realized that I was in a minority on the list, I decided to risk posting a contrasting viewpoint. (I didn't save the correspondence, so this report is from memory and is thus a paraphrase of the cyber-conversation.) No, I said, it's not a good idea for us to develop liturgical rites. It is important that we look for ways to welcome gay and lesbian people into our parishes—indeed, there's never been a time in my priestly or episcopal life when I haven't ministered to gay parishioners—but a liturgical form represents a doctrinal change that would put us at odds with fellow Anglicans around the world and with our ecumenical partners. We should, I concluded, seek opportunities to minister to gay and lesbian people pastorally and to offer all the love and support that we can. But we should avoid taking an irrevocable doctrinal step. My post was (so I thought) mild, irenic, and reasonable.

But the response was overwhelming. "You're a homophobe!" stormed one correspondent. "Don't you realize," asked another, "that it's people like you who cause gay teenagers to commit suicide?" A third gave me some advice: "A fundamentalist like you should leave the Episcopal Church and look for another. We don't need narrow, bigoted people in our church." Lest you think, by the way, that "flaming" is the tactic solely of those on the liberal or progressive side of the church, I should add that I've been "flamed" with equal vehemence by conservatives. One right-wing blogger regularly refers to me as Chicken Little, I imagine because I'm not radical enough for him. ("Blogging" is yet another Internet term; it refers to a "Web log" where people post articles or ideas and others are invited to write responses, often anonymous responses.) Others have called me wobbly, weak-kneed, and a revisionist in conservative clothing. I am enormously thick-skinned, incidentally, and mention these attacks simply to illustrate what's happening in the church. The politics of personal attack have become part of our ecclesiastical culture. J. B. Phillips captures this attitude nicely in his painfully accurate parody of the Beatitudes:

> Happy are the pushers: for they get on in the world.
> Happy are the hard-boiled: for they never let life hurt them.
> Happy are they who complain: for they get their own way in the end.
> Happy are the blasé: for they never worry over their sins.
> Happy are the slave drivers: for they get results.
> Happy are the knowledgeable men of the world: for they know their way around.
> Happy are the troublemakers: for people have to take notice of them.[1]

St. Paul presents a contrast in Philippians. "Rejoice in the Lord always; again I will say, Rejoice. Let your gentleness be known to everyone. The Lord is near" (4:4–5). He begins, of course, by reminding the Philippian Christians (twice!) to rejoice. Joy is never far from Paul's heart. It's the subtext of the letter from beginning to end. Even with Euodia and Syntyche at each other's throats, he encourages his friends to claim the joy, which is his and theirs. Then he turns his attention to the steps they need to take if they are to experience God's peace. The first step, and the subject of this chapter, is *gentleness*.

The word itself (*epieikes* in Greek) defies easy translation. *Epieikes*—which is actually an adjective used as a noun—"denotes seemly, fitting; hence, equitable, fair, moderate, forbearing, not insisting on the letter

---

1. J. B. Phillips, *Your God Is Too Small* (1952; repr. New York: Touchstone, 2004), 92.

of the law; it expresses that considerateness that looks 'humanely and reasonably on the facts of a case.'"[2] While the New Revised Standard Version of the Bible and the New International Version render it as "gentleness," other translations try to tease out other nuances. The Revised English Bible translates *epieikes* as "consideration," the Jerusalem Bible as "tolerance," and the Revised Standard Version as "forbearance." I list these alternatives simply to stress that the word carries a whole range of meanings, a range that can't be captured in any single English expression. Paul uses the word in 2 Corinthians 10:1 to express the character of Jesus himself. "I myself, Paul, appeal to you by the meekness and gentleness of Christ," he says, as he takes the Corinthian Christians to task for decidedly un-Christ-like behavior. The word also appears in the Pastoral Epistles as a way of describing an important quality of the Christian leader. Bishops must be "not violent but gentle" (1 Timothy 3:3); indeed, it's important for all of us "to speak evil of no one, to avoid quarreling, [and] to be gentle" (Titus 3:2). The New Testament era was as contentious as our own (despite the fact that cyberspace didn't exist in the first century!). And so Paul's command that Christians embrace *epieikes* was as countercultural then as it is now.

That leads to a problem, however. The New Testament offers us "power." Jesus' final words, as St. Luke reports them, include the promise that he will empower us. "Stay here in [Jerusalem]," he tells the disciples, "until you are clothed with power from on high" (Luke 24:49). "You will receive power when the Holy Spirit has come upon you," he adds (Acts 1:8). One could understand this promise as the offer of a spiritual big stick. In our culture, after all, power has to do with clout, getting our way, bossing other people around, and winning at all costs. Jim Carey as *Bruce Almighty* provides a picture of what that looks like. He plays a Buffalo, New York, newscaster whose career is on the skids. One night, in despair, he stands on the shore of Lake Ontario, shakes his fist at the sky, and tells God that he could do a better job of running the universe than the Almighty does. God (in the person of Morgan Freeman) takes him up on it. He appears to Bruce and says that, from now on, Bruce will be

---

2. W. E. Vine, *A Comprehensive Dictionary of the Original Greek Words with their Precise Meanings for English Readers* (Peabody, MA: Hendrickson), 484.

the God of Buffalo, New York. Bruce, of course, doesn't believe him—until, later that day, he's sitting in a restaurant and discovers that he can part a bowl of tomato soup, much as Charlton Heston (playing Moses) parts the Red Sea in Cecil B. De Mille's *The Ten Commandments*. Bruce swaggers out of the restaurant, his newfound power a plaything in his hands. He's the God of Buffalo.

The New Testament's picture of power is rather different. Whatever it means, it's not a plaything. It has to do with being a conduit for God's power—and accomplishing God's purposes. When the Gospels report that power emanates from Jesus, the result is invariably healing (see Mark 5:30). Paul himself experienced spiritual power, but always to enhance his ability to preach the good news. "My speech and my proclamation were not with plausible words of wisdom," he tells the Christian community in Corinth, "but with a demonstration of the Spirit and of power, so that your faith might not rest on human wisdom but on the power of God" (1 Corinthians 2:4–5). Power—as the New Testament understands it—isn't a weapon to use on your opponents, but rather a tool to help you to serve Jesus more effectively. And so "power" and "gentleness" aren't opposites. They work together to express the very heart of God.

Our model is Jesus himself. A survey of his ministry reveals remarkable gentleness combined with equally remarkable expressions of spiritual power. Notice, for example, how gently he deals with the woman caught in adultery (John 8:1–11) or the woman with the questionable reputation (Luke 7:36–50). Remember the contrast he draws between the sorrowful tax collector and the self-righteous Pharisee (Luke 18:9–14), commending the tax collector for his repentant heart. Consider his gracious and surprising invitation to Zacchaeus (Luke 19:1–10), another tax collector and one who had apparently extorted funds from the population. Jesus does at times utter harsh words, but they are almost exclusively aimed at the professionally religious (see Matthew 23 as an extended example). He turns over the tables of the money changers (John 2:13–22) and condemns self-satisfied Chorazin and Bethsaida (Matthew 11:21). People who think they've gotten it all together and who look down on those who haven't are the ones singled out for Jesus' wrath. (Maybe this is Jesus' version of a shock treatment, a spiritual "slap in the face.") But ordinary, run-of-the-mill sinners receive unusu-ally gentle treatment. "Come to me, all you that are weary and carrying heavy burdens," Jesus says, "and I will give you rest. Take my yoke upon you and learn from me; for I am gentle and humble in heart, and you will find rest for your souls" (Matthew 11:28–29).

And so Paul's directive expresses the very heart of our Lord. "Let your gentleness be known to everyone. The Lord is near" (Philippians 4:5). When you're pushy, when you try to get your way at all costs, when you do everything in your power to defeat and destroy your opponents—you may well succeed. You may indeed win the day. But God's peace will fly from your heart. On the other hand, when you seek to be gentle, when you're moderate, forbearing, considerate, and reasonable, cutting the other person some slack, recognizing that they, like you, are fallible and broken—then God does a miracle. He grants us "the peace . . . which surpasses all understanding" (4:7) and enables us, even in the midst of chaos, to experience his presence and his love.

What do we need to *do* in order to express the gentleness that Paul urges? That's no small question. Gentleness sounds easy in theory, but finding practical ways of living it out is another matter. My own "train-ing ground" has been the hurly-burly of Episcopal Church politics. As difficult as this era may be, it has had the side benefit of helping me to discover how to be gentle to one's opponents, how to be in relationship with people who stand on the opposite side of very contentious issues. This is a work in progress, filled with potential perils and liable to mis-steps and misunderstandings.

I've discovered that it's important to ascribe to opponents the best possible motives and to assume that they are doing the best that they can to discern the will of God for his church. There's a danger, in any kind of disagreement, to imagine that the people on the other side of issues are acting out of nefarious motives, that they are looking for ways to destroy the church, and that they are conspiring with the forces of militant progressivism (or, from the other perspective, the forces of radi-cal traditionalism) to transform the church into a parody of itself. These are dangerous conclusions indeed. It's better, I've found, to assume the most positive. While another Christian may articulate a vision that (I believe) is inimical to the faith, he or she isn't doing so for the worst of reasons but the best. That makes the conflict more excruciating—no obvious black hats and white hats here—but it also allows us to treat our opponents gently. It's also important to avoid pejorative labels. People on the progressive side tend to dismiss conservatives as fundamentalists or homophobes. People on the conservative side tend to dismiss progressives as revisionists or apostates. (My Internet experience certainly confirms this observation.) Wouldn't it be an improvement to set aside the temptation to label opponents, and to find ways of speaking of them that "respect[s] the dignity of every human being"?[3] Paul does at times use intemperate language (e.g., 3:2; Galatians 1:8–9); but perhaps he's urging gentleness in Philippians 4:4–5 as a kind of self-correction, balancing out his earlier words and offering an alternative way to deal with opponents.

The problem with a specific example, of course, is that it can detract from the general principle. So my reference to the struggles in the Episcopal Church may provide as much distraction as enlightenment. (If that's the case, feel free to ignore the preceding paragraph!) The challenge for every Christian—the challenge that St. Paul throws down in his concise but difficult directive—is to find ways of living gently, wherever God has put us. The "wherever" cuts a broad swath: the workplace, school, church, neighborhood, politics, our families and households. In each arena, we meet difficult people (remembering that others consider *us* the ones who are difficult). In each arena, we need to find ways to disagree without rancor, to articulate our own deeply held convictions without destroying or dehumanizing people on the other side. Is such a thing possible? Perhaps our greatest asset is another Christian who can model gentleness for us. Mine was John Kimball Saville.

I mentioned in Chapter Nine that I served two curacies (assistantships) before becoming a rector with a parish of my own. The second curacy—at St. Michael's in Anaheim, California—put me under the care of Father Saville. He was my boss, my supervisor, my trainer—and my mentor. More than anything else, he taught me to be gentle. I arrived at St. Michael's in 1973, twenty-six years old, ordained just two years,

---

3. *Book of Common Prayer* (New York: Oxford University Press, 1979), 305.

dreadfully self-important, with just enough training and experience to be very, very dangerous. Looking back from a distance of almost three and a half decades, I still cringe with embarrassment when I remember my certainty, my unshakable conviction that I knew what the church needed to do to fix its ills, and my utter disdain of people who weren't on board with my insights. Kim (as Father Saville was known to his friends) bravely undertook the assignment of taming an unruly ecclesiastical neophyte. Sometimes I wonder why he didn't fire me. (In retrospect, *I* would have fired me!) I tried to reform the parish liturgy, revamp its administrative infrastructure, retool the Christian education program, and reinvent its mission strategy—and not, mind you, with any subtlety. Week after week at staff meetings, I ranted, raved, and complained. In the face of this spiritual firestorm, Kim remained remarkably calm. Sometimes he allowed me to experiment (even when he knew that the experimentation would inevitably lead to failure). Sometimes he gently corrected me (but always one-on-one and behind closed doors). Sometimes he simply listened and smiled and nodded. I remember an incident in which I'd managed to offend a parish matriarch (the details are long forgotten, but the matriarch's anger isn't); Kim helped me to find the courage to go to her and apologize. Time after time, though I was often unaware of it, Kim saved my pastoral bacon. When I left St. Michael's after almost three years under his care, my life had been gently shaped and transformed.

Kim died just a few months before this book was written. A couple of years earlier, I had the opportunity to visit him at the retirement community where he and his wife Nellie lived and to thank him for the powerful way that he'd touched my life. Kim taught me to be gentle, and I will always be grateful to him and for him.

In many ways, Philippians 4:5 may be the most difficult challenge that St. Paul ever issued. The words look at first glance like a throwaway line; and many a preacher has quickly moved on to the next (and more familiar) verses. But, in fact, this command has real "bite." Paul wrote these words in the specific context of intrachurch conflict (Euodia and Syntyche) and in the wider setting of the struggle among the first Christians about the Torah. Be gentle with one another, he reminds his friends in Philippi. Remember that the Lord is near: Jesus himself, who dealt so very gently with sinners and who reserved his condemnation for the self-righteousness; Jesus himself, who deals so gently with *you*, and invites you to do the same with one another.

Questions for Reflection

1. How have you experienced Jesus' gentleness in your own life?

2. Who has modeled gentleness for you? Who has shown you how to be gentle with others, even with the most difficult people?

3. Can you think of a time when someone was gentle with you, when perhaps you least deserved it?

4. What are the situations now where Jesus is asking you to be gentle? To cut others some slack?

CHAPTER 12

Pray

Philippians 4:6–7

The most unusual icon in my office is an ugly block of concrete. It sits on a shelf behind my desk, flanked by an icon of the Blessed Virgin on one side and an icon of the ascended and reigning Christ on the other. Why the concrete?

When I was fifteen years old and a convinced atheist, my mother introduced me to an elderly friend—a Russian émigré who had come to the United States in the 1920s, fleeing the Communist regime that had expropriated her family's property and killed many of her relatives. While I can no longer remember her name, I can still, in my mind's eye, see her face and hear her voice. She told me about life in Russia before the revolution and about the privileges that she enjoyed as an aristocrat: a mansion in Moscow and a mansion in the country, servants, and a constant round of social activities. All that was swept away in 1917, and, in the ensuing years, this woman had found (or, more accurately, been found by) God. Her Orthodox faith was deep but (from my atheistic perspective) naïve and simplistic. Eventually, after escaping from Russia, she'd made her way across the Atlantic, married a wealthy American businessman, and now lived in Manhattan, regaling friends at dinner parties with tales of the old Russia and her hopes for the future. One night at dinner she told me that she prayed every day for the downfall of the Soviet Union and the reconversion of her home-land. I remember thinking, "This woman is *nuts*! The Soviet Union is impregnable. Nothing will change that—and especially saying prayers. How pathetic!"

Almost forty years later, a friend returned from a trip to several for-mer Eastern bloc nations and brought me a gift: a small, jagged piece of concrete that he took from a torn-down section of the Berlin Wall. The concrete now sits among my icons, an outward sign that no prayer is pathetic, that God hears the prayers of his people, that God is infinitely capable of overturning empires and changing the inexorable course of history. Every time I look at the concrete, I remember with gratitude that elderly Russian émigré and her faithful prayers. She—in company with countless others—helped to bring down the Soviet Union and its allies. Her prayers cooperated with the very purposes of God.

When St. Paul encourages his friends in Philippi to pray, he's giving them both a very easy and a very hard command. On the one hand, there's nothing easier than to say, "Please." Prayer does not need to be complicated. There's no requirement that our prayers be offered in Eliz-abethan cadences, nor do they have to be theologically sophisticated. Sometimes the best and most heartfelt prayer is the simplest and most direct: "Help!" On the other hand, Christians struggle with prayer all their lives. More than thirty-five years of pastoral experience have con-vinced me that prayer is the single most pressing problem for Chris-tians. How should I pray? What should I pray? How can I pray when my mind is a jumble of fears and longings, hopes and worries? Chris-tians often wonder if it's possible to bring their prayer life into some kind of coherent order. With so much psychic competition, prayer can present apparently insurmountable problems.

Paul is aware of all of this interior confusion, and so he begins the section on prayer with a realistic acknowledgment of the problem. "Do not be worried about anything" (Philippians 4:6a), he says. The com-mand could rightly be translated (as in other versions), "Do not be anxious." The Greek verb *merimnao* has to do with being drawn in dif-ferent directions, a reference to internal distractions; and that, certainly, is in the very nature of anxiety. It can seem at times as though there's an endless loop tape playing in our minds, the same material repeating itself over and over and over. The content of the tape, naturally, varies from person to person. For one, it might have to do with health; for another, finances; for another, interpersonal conflict; for another, worries about family or friends or the state of the church. Whatever the distraction, the principle is the same. Paul himself was no stranger to this painful phenomenon. "Besides other things," he tells the church in Corinth, "I am under daily pressure because of my anxiety for all the churches" (2 Corinthians 11:28). While none of us carries an apostolic burden comparable to Paul's, we can imagine how difficult it was for him to pray. In letter after letter, he's putting out fires, trying to bring his unruly churches into some degree of order, correcting errors. He, like his friends in Philippi, must have felt himself pulled in different directions.

That means that Paul may well have been writing as much for himself as for his Philippian parishioners. "Do not worry about anything," he says, and then continues, "but in everything by prayer and supplication with thanksgiving let your request be made known to God" (4:6). This compact direction contains some very specific words about developing a life of prayer in the face of debilitating distractions. To begin with, Paul uses two words for prayer, one general and one particular. The general word *proseuche* refers to the overall process of praying. You do this when you simply place yourself consciously in the presence of God. It may or may not involve words. Thanksgiving, confession, intercession, praise, meditation, and contemplation are all included under the heading of *proseuche*, and when you pray you may do all, some, or none of these things. Thomas Green, SJ, in his primer on prayer titled *Opening to God*, tells the story of Jimmy, a laborer who, at the end of the workday, would come into church, sit for several minutes, and then leave. The parish priest, seeing Jimmy day after day, could not contain himself and eventually asked the question, What are you doing here? "Nothing much, Father. I just say, 'Jesus, it's Jimmy.' And he says, 'Jimmy, it's Jesus.' And we're very happy together."[1] In other words, prayer does not necessarily *accomplish* anything, at least anything of

---

1. Thomas Greene, SJ, *Opening to God* (Notre Dame, IN: Ave Maria Press, 1977) 19.

immediate benefit. When you pray, you're hanging out with God, and that's a sufficient end in itself.

The second word, *deesis*, has a narrower focus. The New Revised Standard Version of the Bible translates it as "supplication," and that captures something of the flavor. It has to do with bringing particular requests to God's attention. (More about whether he actually *needs* to be told in the next paragraph.) Paul says that we rid ourselves of anxiety by turning over to God the source of those anxieties, presenting him our supplications. Paul doesn't prescribe a specific set of words for doing so. He doesn't tell us, for instance, how detailed to make our prayers. Must we delineate all known symptoms of a disease, or is it sufficient just to say, "Jesus, please heal Harry," leaving the rest to him? While Paul provides no formula, we do have Jesus' own words on this matter: "When you are praying, do not heap up empty phrases as the Gentiles do; for they think that they will be heard because of their many words" (Matthew 6:7). Whatever level of detail is appropriate, both Paul and Jesus urge us to bring our deepest concerns to God, to place them in the Father's care, and to leave both the results and the timing to him. In the end, prayer is a costly and risky letting-go.

Perhaps the strangest phrase in this section involves the process of prayer: "Let your requests be made known to God" (4:6b). After all, in the passage from the Sermon on the Mount cited in the preceding paragraph, Jesus goes on to say, "Do not be like [the Gentiles], for your Father knows what you need before you ask him" (Matthew 6:8). Is God surprised by our prayers? Hardly! Jesus makes it clear that our requests don't catch the Father off guard, as if he slaps himself on the knee and says, "My goodness, I didn't know that Harriet has a bum back!" (I understand that I'm speaking anthropomorphically.) We're encountering here one of the great mysteries of the Christian faith, the interplay between our free will on the one hand and God's omniscience and providence on the other. Free will is indicated by the fact that we bother to pray at all rather than simply wait for things to happen. Omniscience and providence affirm the reality that God knows everything and is in charge of everything. *Both* are true. It isn't necessary, in fact, for us to work this out. We know, as a matter of obedience, that the scriptures urge us to pray. A quick glance at any biblical concordance will reveal passage after passage, in both Testaments, regarding the importance of prayer. At the same time, even a superficial jaunt through the same scriptures reminds us that the "earth is the Lord's, and all that is in it" (Psalm 24:1). And so the mystery is this: the all-powerful God—who does not need our prayer—invites us to pray, and thereby cooperate with his purposes.

Many years ago, when I served as rector of St. Joseph's Church in Buena Park, California, I led a Bible study on Tuesday evenings that drew a surprisingly large number of parishioners (Episcopalians are not famed for their avid Bible reading; happily, St. Joseph's gave the lie to that generalization!). I'm not especially skilled at group process, and so the Bible study's methodology was fairly simple: lecture, combined with questions and answers. Over the course of eight or nine years, we covered large chunks of the scriptures, and Tuesday night became a spiritual high point of my week. It was, to be sure, an exhausting addition to my schedule. The preparation and the teaching took an enormous amount of time and energy, though I never, not even for one moment, regretted the output. At the end of an evening's teaching, however, I would usually be drained, exhausted, and ready to escape and go home.

One Tuesday night, the lecture and the questions done, Art and Sally came up to me with their adult daughter, Frances. "Father Ed, could you please pray for Frances?" Art asked. "She's been diagnosed with grand mal epilepsy." I already knew much of the story. Frances had been a successful and creative business person, with a career on the rise in the public-relations field. Suddenly and without warning, she began to experience seizures, major ones, and her life quickly unraveled. Her doctor put her on Phenobarbital, a powerful medication with debilitating side effects, she lost her driver's license, she could no longer commute to work, and ultimately she had to give up her job. Over the course of just a few weeks, a strong and confident young woman found herself alone, terrified, and hopeless. And so Art and Sally came to me that Tuesday night and asked me to pray for their daughter.

I must confess that I was unprepared for their request. At the end of an evening of teaching, I was drained. (This may be the result of my strong introversion. People like me can often function quite well in public settings. We appear witty, insightful, and energetic; but when the work is done, we need to get away from crowds and recharge—in solitude.) When Art and Sally approached me, my first thought (blessedly unarticulated, but that doesn't excuse me) was, "Oh no!" I had no energy left for anyone or anything, and especially for a task as important as intercessory prayer for a seriously ill woman. My body ached and my mind was numb. And yet, of course, duty required a response. I agreed to pray for Frances, and her parents and I went into the church. Frances knelt at the altar rail. Then, more in irritation and frustration than in devotion, I put my hands on her head and said, "Oh God, make Frances well. Amen." That was it, all that I could (or would) manage. St. James talks about the "prayer of faith [saving] the sick" (James 5:15). What I offered Frances, though, was light years from James's ideal, perhaps more a "prayer of annoyance." Frances got up from the altar rail, and she and her parents left. It was as unanointed a moment as one might imagine.

Except, she was healed. I didn't find out until some months later that Frances's symptoms suddenly and without explanation stopped. The doctors waited for the symptoms to resume; and when, finally, they didn't, they took her off Phenobarbital. Eventually, Frances reclaimed both her driver's license and her career. Whatever happened that night, it had nothing to do with me. My prayer for Frances had been accompanied by neither eloquent words nor spiritual fervor. God didn't need them. I should add that the last time I saw Frances—some years after this experience—she had embarked on a new career. She's now a youth pastor.

Paul goes on to make a promise. "And the peace of God, which surpasses all understanding, will guard your hearts and your minds in Christ Jesus" (Philippians 4:7). The problem with this phrase is that the word "peace" conjures up for us intonations absent from the Greek (and Hebrew) word. We tend to think of peace as the absence of conflict. Thus, on Sunday, most churches pray for peace in the world's trouble spots. Neville Chamberlain, returning from Munich in 1938, waved a piece of paper in the air and announced, "There will be peace in our time"—by which he meant no war; he was, of course, tragically wrong. The scriptures mean something rather different. Jesus himself, preparing his disciples for his departure (both near-term on Good Friday and long-term on Ascension Day), speaks of peace but not the cessation of conflict. "Peace I leave with you," he says. "My peace I give to you. I do not give to you as the world gives" (John 14:27). And then he adds, "I have said this to you, so that in me you may have peace. In the world you face persecution. But take courage; I have conquered the world!" (John 16:33). The peace that Jesus offers us neither protects us from persecution nor isolates us from conflict.

"When it was evening on that day, the first day of the week, and the doors of the house where the disciples had met were locked for fear of the Jews, Jesus came and stood among them and said, 'Peace be with you.' After he had said this, he showed them his hands and his side" (John 20:19–20). I've always been struck by the fact that on the first Easter night Jesus combines the standard Hebrew greeting, common among Jews of his day and our own, with a grim reminder of the marks of his death. Whatever peace he offers, it is intertwined with his suffering. Christ's peace "will guard your hearts and your minds," a military analogy that calls to mind a sentinel watching over us, keeping us safe: not from conflict or even from failure and death, but from anything that would separate us from God and from one another. In the end, the "peace . . . which surpasses understanding" means that Jesus invites us into a right relationship both with himself and with brothers and sisters, a relationship that doesn't depend on outward circumstances or even an inner tranquility. Peace is a fact, not a feeling. No matter what, we belong to him. No matter what, he links us to one another. He is in charge of the big picture.

As I mentioned in Chapter 6, the period following the General Convention of 2003 was a time of turmoil in my life—a turmoil that was shared by virtually everyone in leadership in the Episcopal Church, indeed by countless ordinary Episcopalians. No matter where one stood on the difficult issue of human sexuality, there was no escaping the pain and confusion that the Convention generated. Day after day, I answered hundreds of e-mails, wrote dozens of letters, and responded to angry telephone calls, a relentless outpouring of anxiety.

In the midst of the uproar, Jean (a former parishioner from Bakersfield) sent me a card. It simply contained some words spoken by the Lord to the exiled Jews in Babylon, hundreds of years before the birth of

Jesus. The exiles languished hopelessly in a foreign city, no end in view, no way home. The prophet Jeremiah—among a minority left behind in Jerusalem—wrote to them, a letter of comfort and hope, including this: "For surely I know the plans I have for you, says the Lord, plans for your welfare and not for harm, to give you a future and a hope" (Jeremiah 29:11). As I read the Lord's words through Jeremiah, offered in a very different context, I knew that they were written for me as well. I had no end in view, no way out. (I still don't, to be honest.) That's OK. The future is in God's hands, not mine. I find myself thinking about the prayer popularly ascribed to Pope John XXIII. Just before turning in at the end of the day, Pope John would pray, "Lord, it's your church. I'm going to bed." Jean's card helped me to reframe a most painful season and, at least for a time, to pray good Pope John's prayer.

And so Paul's instruction—"Do not worry about anything" (4:6)—doesn't mean that life will work out the way that we desire or that there will be "a happy issue out of all [our] afflictions."[2] Not all stories end like Frances's, however fervently we pray. But Paul articulates a promise infinitely more glorious. The God of the Universe invites us to pray: to bring to his attention the deepest concerns of our hearts. He knows them already, yet he yearns for us to offer those concerns to him. In doing so, he promises another infinite gift, a peace that is well more than the cessation of conflict or the balm of inner tranquility, a peace rooted in the life, death, and resurrection of our Lord Jesus Christ.

QUESTIONS FOR REFLECTION

1. What tends to trigger anxiety in you? How do you experience the interior distractions that anxiety generates?

2. What enhances your ability to bring your concerns to the Lord in prayer? What gets in the way?

---

2. *Book of Common Prayer* (New York: Oxford University Press, 1979), 815.

3. Can you think of a time when you experienced the "peace of God, which surpasses all understanding," despite outward circumstances?

4. What challenges do you face today as you seek to claim God's peace?

CHAPTER 13

Think

Philippians 4:8–9

My family and I lived for almost fourteen years in the "country music capital of the West"—Bakersfield, California. The country music industry was well-established in the town, a number of well-known country singers (e.g., Buck Owens and Merle Haggard) had grown up there, and country music stations filled the radio dial. During our time in Bakersfield, the city renamed a major street "Buck Owens Boulevard." And so, virtually out of necessity, I became something of a fan of country music. Since I couldn't escape it, I decided, I might as well enjoy it.

Enjoy it I did; the beat and the tunes energized me; but after a few years I began to notice that when country music was playing, I'd start to feel—well, sad. My mood would darken, my shoulders would droop, and I could sense a kind of heaviness coming over me. What was going on? The tunes, after all, were rather upbeat. Finally, I realized that the problem wasn't the music, it was the lyrics. After all, many country music songs deal with tragic themes: you smash up your pickup truck, mama dies, your woman leaves you for a rodeo cowboy, you get drunk and the police throw you in jail, you hop a freight train to escape your troubles. The lyrics are as troubling and depressing as any Shakespearean tragedy. I discovered that after several years of listening to these sorrowful songs, they were having an impact—a negative impact—on my interior life. As much as I delighted in the tunes and the beat and the country music ambience, I had to set my radio to the one classical station in town and listen to country only occasionally (and very sparingly).

All of which led me to rediscover an important biblical principle: What you put into your brain will have a significant effect on your mood, your behavior, and ultimately your relationship with the Lord. It will determine your attitude, your actions, and your willingness to follow Jesus. Our ability to experience "the peace of God, which surpasses all understanding" (Philippians 4:7) will depend to a large extent upon what we choose to allow into our hearts and minds.

As he continues to reflect on God's peace, St. Paul turns to this very reality. "Finally, beloved, whatever is true, whatever is honorable, whatever is just, whatever is pure, whatever is pleasing, whatever is commendable, if there is any excellence and if there is anything worthy of praise, think about these things. Keep on doing the things that you have learned and received and seen in me, and the God of peace will be with you" (4:8–9). Paul is talking here about the relationship between our thought life and our behavior, and he is urging his friends in Philippi to take great care about the former in order to enhance the latter. If your thought life is out of control, he's saying, you will drift away from godly conduct. On the other hand, if you remain vigilant about what enters your heart and mind, it will enable you more faithfully to follow Jesus and to encounter the peace that the Lord yearns to give his people. Paul makes this point by offering two important principles.

First, he tells the Christians in Philippi to consider carefully what they allow into their minds, and he supplies something of a "laundry list" of virtues to make the point. We're to think about whatever is true, honorable, just, pure, pleasing (most translations render the word as "lovely" or "loveable"), commendable, excellent, and praiseworthy. Obviously, these are general terms; but the point Paul makes is that we should be intentional about our thought life. What enters our minds will inevitably have an effect on us, either negative or positive.

Our own experience confirms this principle. We live in an era in which we are constantly bombarded by information. Data comes to us from newspapers, radio, television, the Internet, and e-mail. The information may be true or it may be false, but in either case it has an impact on us. We can't prevent it from doing so. Consider, for example, the phenomenon of "urban legends." I regularly receive e-mails—generally in the form of forwarded material—warning me of some dreadful plot. One claims that the Procter and Gamble logo is actually a satanic symbol. Another urges me to sign an Internet petition because atheist Madeleine Murray O'Hare has asked the Federal Communications Commission to ban religious broadcasting. Still, another warns that family violence increases exponentially during the Super Bowl, as testosterone is released all over the country. It happens that all of these are false. (I even found a Web site that lists urban legends and refutes them. Mrs. O'Hare, to give one example, is actually long dead). But it's possible, reading one warning after another after another, to have one's mind unconsciously shaped and formed in a disastrous way so that we see the world through a conspiratorial lens. That, in turn, can lead to attitudes and behaviors that make it difficult for us to trust people (even the most trustworthy) or to trust God himself. All of this, of course, may well occur unconsciously. We're not aware that our hearts and minds are being transformed.

And so Paul is asking his friends in Philippi to consider another way of filling their minds. The word that translates "think" (*logizomai*) is stronger and more forceful than its English equivalent. It has to do with pondering, reflecting, making these subjects (whatever is true, honorable, just, etc.) the object of our careful thought, internalizing them. Elsewhere, Paul talks about this process under the heading of spiritual formation. "'For who has known the mind of the Lord so as to instruct him?'" he asks rhetorically, quoting the book of Job; and then he answers his own question: "But we have the mind of Christ" (1 Corinthians 2:16). In other words, through the Spirit we are empowered to think the very thoughts of Jesus. Christ is "formed" in us (see Galatians 4:19).

Scripture is the principle tool as we seek the mind of Christ. We read the Bible not simply to gather information about the people of Israel, the early church, or Jesus himself (though the Bible contains a good deal of information, much of it both enlightening and fascinating), nor do we read it merely for its literary or even its devotional merits (though the Bible is unmatched in beauty and unequaled in its ability to inspire and ennoble its readers). Rather, we read the Bible primarily so that we can get to know God better. In these texts, he reveals his character, his purposes, and his will for our lives. Above all, he reveals the Son of God, "who loved me and gave himself for me" (Galatians 2:20). Slowly, over time, as these ancient words take root in us, we come to know the mind of Christ. A collect in the *Book of Common Prayer* describes the process: "Almighty God, who caused all holy Scriptures to be written for our learning: Grant us so to hear them, read, mark, learn, and inwardly digest them, that we may embrace and ever hold fast the blessed hope of everlasting life, which you have given us in our Savior Jesus Christ, who lives and reigns with you and the Holy Spirit, one God, for ever and ever. *Amen.*"[1]

This occurs on two levels. In part, specific texts speak to specific situations. For example, should I rob the First National Bank? Happily, a particular text (Exodus 20:15) applies and gives me helpful and unmistakable direction. On the other hand, some questions are more general. What is the Lord's purpose for my life? How is Jesus calling me to follow him? Those questions invite us to encounter the Bible on another level, looking not so much at specific texts but at the general flow of the story of redemption. As I "hear, read, mark, learn, and inwardly digest" the story, what does it tell me about God's character? What does it reveal about his intentions for humankind, and how might he be asking me to make myself available to cooperate with those purposes? In other words, how does the Bible unveil the mind of Christ? Christians spend a lifetime pondering the scriptures—for they supremely disclose what is true, honorable, and just—and allowing them to sink in, to make a home in us.

Here's a test. Imagine that you are driving alone on a relatively uncrowded freeway. You are, of course, paying attention to the road; but it's a stress-free drive, you've turned off the radio, and your mind is free to wander wherever it will. The question is, where does it go? Do you find yourself thinking about your fears, your angers, or your ambitions? Do

---

1. *Book of Common Prayer* (New York: Oxford University Press, 1979), 236.

Think

you ponder old grudges? Do you create mental scenarios in which you brilliantly refute your critics? Or, on the other hand, do you ask yourself questions about Jesus and your call to discipleship? Do you consider what he wants of your life? Do you reflect on how you can serve him better? When left to your own devices, with nothing to distract you, you get a good indication about what's really important in your heart and mind. Where does your mind go in a kind of "free-float" state? Paul challenges us to be as intentional as possible in pondering whatever will draw us into the heart of Jesus.

Second, Paul tells his friends in Philippi to allow their most godly thoughts to shape their behavior. "Keep on doing the things that you have learned and received and heard and seen in me" (4:9). He encourages them—and us—to make a conscious connection between what we're thinking and what we're doing. This won't happen accidentally. Just as we have to be intentional about what goes in, we have to be equally intentional about what comes out. The *Book of Common Prayer*, in its baptismal liturgy, has a helpful way of expressing this dynamic. Just before the candidates are baptized, the congregation prays a litany (a series of short prayers with a set response). The verbs tell the tale:

> Deliver them, O Lord, from the way of sin and death. *Lord, hear our prayer.*
> Open their hearts to your grace and truth. *Lord, hear our prayer.*
> Fill them with your holy and life-giving Spirit. *Lord, hear our prayer.*
> Keep them in the faith and communion of your holy Church. *Lord, hear our prayer.*
> Teach them to love others in the power of the Spirit. *Lord, hear our prayer.*
> Send them into the world in witness to your love. *Lord, hear our prayer.*
> Bring them to the fullness of your peace and glory. *Lord, hear our prayer.*[2]

The prayer begins with the transformation of the heart. It moves on to transformation of behavior. The one without the other is incomplete. I

---

2. Ibid., 305.

once heard Father Terry Fullam, rector all of St. Paul's in Darien, Connecticut, and a leader in spiritual renewal in the 1970s, put this principle most colorfully: "The fruit of the Spirit only grow in the garden of obedience."

Paul reminds his friends that "primary data" in this process is the example of others. We saw in Chapter 10 that Paul didn't hesitate to ask people to imitate him (see Philippians 3:17), not as a way of boosting his self-esteem but in recognition of the fact that we learn to follow Jesus by watching other people following Jesus. Jesus himself employed that method. His disciples accompanied him on his journeys, watched him in action as he taught and healed, and then—for instance, in Luke 9:1–2—tried it out for themselves. The principle is clear: we need others to teach us to be faithful. Thus, it was that Jay showed me how a Christian dies.

Jay and his wife, Kathy, had been longtime members of one of the smaller parishes in the diocese. As often happens in small congregations, he'd rotated through virtually all lay ministry positions—acolyte, usher, Lay Eucharistic Minister, vestry member, treasurer, clerk, junior warden, senior warden. One day Jay's priest called me and told me that Jay had been diagnosed with brain cancer and had only a few weeks to live. Would I be willing to pay a visit? Of course, I replied. Not long afterward, I knocked on Jay and Kathy's door, and Kathy brought me into the room where Jay lay dying. The brain cancer had affected his speech centers, and he was no longer able to talk coherently. I could tell by the twinkle in his eye that he recognized me and understood what I was saying; but when he tried to respond, what came out was a kind of "word salad," utterly incomprehensible. My conversation was primarily directed toward Kathy, though Jay nodded and smiled throughout. When it was time to leave, I offered to pray. Again, Jay nodded. Since I stood on his left side, I took his left hand in mine, while Kathy stood on his right and put her hand on his shoulder. I began to pray. As I did so, Jay reached out with his right hand and placed it on my head, a dying man blessing his bishop. He now, with Esther (as we saw in Chapter 1) and countless others whom it has been my privilege to serve, sees Jesus face-to-face and continues to pray for his friends. My deepest hope is that I die as faithfully and lovingly as my friend Jay.

The challenge for Christians, Paul is saying, is to find ways of linking thought and action. "Only he who believes is obedient," says Dietrich Bonhoeffer, "and only he who is obedient believes."[3] When the interior and exterior of our lives meet in a seamless whole, "the God of peace will be with you" (Philippians 4:9). Joining the two is often a painfully difficult exercise.

The Japanese author Shesaku Endo wrote a powerful novel set in the early seventeenth century, a time when persecution lashed out against Christians and drove the church underground for hundreds of years. *The Samurai* tells the story of Rokeumon Hasekura, a low-level soldier who is sent with two others on an economic and diplomatic mission to Mexico and, ultimately, to Spain and Italy. The Japanese government hopes to begin establishing ties to the West, and Hasekura's task is to negotiate with the Spanish government and to open the doors to economic exchange. Accompanying the three samurais is an ambitious Franciscan priest who convinces them that the only way their mission can be successful is if the Japanese travelers submit to Christian baptism. That will win them credibility and open doors for them. Reluctantly, and without faith, the three agree and are baptized. The priest's ploy fails, however. European officials see through the sham conversions, and the diplomatic mission is unable to accomplish its goal. The samurais return to Japan in disgrace.

What's worse, when they get home, the political tide has turned. The Japanese government now sees the church as a threat and has embarked on a program of systematic persecution. Hasekura faces death on behalf of a faith that he doesn't believe. As he awaits execution, in his mind's eye he returns to Mexico, where he and his companions would often stay in Christian monasteries. (No motels in seventeenth-century Mexico!) There, on the monastic wall, he would stare in confusion at the crucifix, the tortured Jesus hanging in agony. How could Christians worship such a powerless god? How could such a symbol do anything but repel? But now, preparing for death, Hasekura is haunted by the crucified Christ; and slowly, over time, a peace comes upon him. He

---

3. Dietrich Bonhoeffer, *The Cost of Discipleship* (1937; New York: Touchstone, 1995), 63.

lived Paul's principle in reverse: first the outward sign, then the interior belief, the seamless whole in the face of death. Walking, almost by accident, the way of the cross, he remembers the words of another Japanese Christian and, in that memory, comes to faith:

> He is always beside us.
> He listens to our agony and our grief
> He weeps with us.
> And He says to us,
> "Blessed are they who weep in this life,
> for in the kingdom of heaven they shall smile."[4]

As for Hasekura, for Paul, and for us, the seamless whole transforms us. "The peace of God . . . will guard your hearts and your minds in Christ Jesus . . . The God of peace will be with you" (4:7, 9). The challenge for all of us is twofold. First, we need to discover ways that we can internalize spiritual realities, not as a kind of vague spirituality, but with Christian specificity. Inevitably, the process will be different for each of us. Temperament, personality, and particular circumstances will all have an impact. Parents of young children—stressed for time alone, exhausted, unable to find a quite spot from first light to lights out—face a challenge very different from, say, retired people with a good deal of open space and flexibility. The "rule of life" (an old term referring to one's chosen spiritual disciplines) may be simple or complex, multifaceted or monofocused.

Second, we need to be willing to ask ourselves hard questions about the connections we make between what is in our heart and how we live our lives. Sometimes the Spirit provides instant and painful insight. For example, I remember, when I became a parent, that I made a series of "I will never" statements. "I will never . . . scream irrationally at my children," recalling of course some difficult childhood experiences of my own. In the nanosecond that followed the first time that I screamed irrationally at my child, it felt as though the Holy Spirit called up my resolution and said, "See?" It was a horrible but salutary moment. More

---

4. Shesaku Endo, *The Samurai* (New York: New Directions, 1982), 242.

often, however, we make those discoveries slowly, over time, as our hearts and minds are able to deal with the information. Discipleship, after all, is a lifelong process of learning, growing, and finding ways to incarnate our faith in daily life. We shouldn't expect, and probably could not handle, the full disclosure of the dark places that inhabit our hearts. Even a partial revelation is enough to spur us on and to encourage us to follow Jesus. We are, after all, infinitely precious to him, chosen "before the foundation of the world to be holy and blameless before him in love" (Ephesians 1:4). As imperfect yet beloved disciples, St. Paul invites us to "think about these things" and to "keep on doing the things that you have learned" (Philippians 4:8–9).

QUESTIONS FOR REFLECTION

1. When your mind is free to "float free" (e.g., when driving alone on an uncrowded road), what do you find yourself thinking about?

2. What is the best way for you to be intentional about your thought life? How do you see to it that your spiritual input includes "whatever is true"?

3. Can you think of a time when you were able to make a connection between the faith as it resides in your heart and an action that you performed? How did you make that connection?

4. The Philippian Christians had Paul as their model of discipleship. Who is yours?

CHAPTER 14

Give

Philippians 4:10–20

"*I do, and with God's grace I will follow him as my Savior and Lord!*"
I put these words in italics because Jeff uttered them so forcefully. He was young for a confirmation candidate, only twelve or thirteen, but his priest thought him ready to make a public commitment to Jesus Christ. A couple of days before my visit, however, Jeff shattered his leg as he skateboarded. Apparently, he was attempting some sort of fly-through-the-air maneuver, ended up doing an unintentional 360-degree flip, and landed in an awkward heap. His tibia was multiply fractured, no small matter when you're in the middle of an adolescent growth spurt. The doctors pieced his bone back together, bound him up in a cast, and ordered him to stay at home for six weeks, all of which prevented him from being confirmed at the appointed time in his parish church.

Jeff's priest called and asked if I'd be willing to confirm him in his living room following the Eucharist at church. Of course, I happily agreed to do so. On Sunday morning, following the Eucharist and a parish potluck, we made our way to Jeff's home. I was unprepared for the extent to which the cast had immobilized him. The plaster extended from mid-calf to mid-chest, and Jeff was semireclining in a wheelchair made especially for people with injuries as severe as his. He could move his arms and his head but was otherwise frozen in place. I gave him a copy of the *Book of Common Prayer*, explained the liturgy to him, and began the service. When we came to the confirmation vows, I asked two questions prescribed in the Prayer Book:

> So you reaffirm your renunciation of evil?
> I do.
> Do you renew your commitment to Jesus Christ?
> I do, and with God's grace I will follow him as my Savior and Lord.[1]

Jeff virtually shouted out those last words. I don't think I've ever heard a confirmand reply with such enthusiasm and grit. His fervor was all the more amazing because Jeff wasn't, at that moment, capable of doing anything at all. He was stuck—not in the stocks like Paul, but in a body cast—fastened in place, unable to scratch an itch or take care of his most basic needs. And yet he yielded himself to Jesus without reservation and told him that, no matter what, he belonged to the Lord. He offered Jesus a blank check and invited him to write on it what he will. Jeff said, in effect, Wherever you lead me, Lord, I will follow, though I don't yet know the destination. Whatever you ask me to do, I will obey, though you have not yet revealed your will for my life.

When I laid hands on Jeff and anointed him with oil, I knew that my words and his were utterly congruent. "Strengthen, O Lord, your servant Jeff with your Holy Spirit; empower him for your service; and sustain him all the days of his life."[2]

St. Paul's friends in Philippi also offered Jesus a blank check. For them, the check was in fact literal, a gift of money. As we saw briefly in the prologue, the Letter to the Philippians is an extended thank-you note. The Philippian Christians had gotten word of Paul's imprisonment and sent one of their own, Epaphroditus, to minister to Paul in prison and to bring him a monetary gift for his support (Philippians 2:25). During the journey, however, Epaphroditus took ill, and Paul sent him back to Philippi as quickly as possible, lest his Philippian friends be consumed with worry over the fate of their messenger. "I am the more eager to send him, therefore, in order that you may rejoice at

---

1. *Book of Common Prayer* (New York: Oxford University Press, 1979), 415.
2. Ibid., 418.

seeing him again, and that I may be less anxious. Welcome him then in the Lord with all joy, and honor such people, because he came close to death for the work of Christ, risking his life to make up for those service that you could not give me" (2:28–30). At the end of the letter, pondering "the peace of God, which surpasses all understanding" (4:7), Paul returns to the Philippians' gift, and reflects in depth on their generosity—and God's.

Paul begins, nor surprisingly, with a final word of joy. "I rejoice in the Lord greatly," he says, "that now at last you have revived your concern for me; indeed, you were concerned for me, but had no opportunity to show it" (4:10). He goes on in his concluding paragraphs to reflect on what this gift of money means: for Paul as the recipient, for the Philippian Christians as the givers, and for all of us as we consider our life as disciples of Jesus Christ. Paul does so in three ways.

First, he tells his friends, remember that God is generous. "Not that I am referring to being in need," Paul emphasizes, "for I have learned to be content with whatever I have. I know what it is to have little, and I know what it is to have plenty. In any and all circumstances I have learned the secret of being well-fed and of going hungry, of having plenty and of being in need. I can do all things through him who strengthens me" (4:11–13). Paul takes the long view. Looking back over his life, his missionary journeys, and the hardships he's endured for the sake of the gospel, he sees God's generosity at work. No matter what, the Lord has provided for him—sometimes plentifully, sometimes less so, but always sufficiently. Even in times of scarcity, God has made available whatever Paul needed in order to follow Jesus effectively. Paul is testifying to the Lord's absolute faithfulness. Whenever Jesus calls us, he always empowers. He never gives us a task without also supplying the resources and the spiritual power to accomplish it. But Paul is careful to engage in "truth in advertising." God's provision does not necessarily mean riches. Whether there's much or little, it's always enough.

Once again, Paul is countercultural. We live in an acquisitive age. We measure our success and, perhaps, even our worth in terms of the resources we accumulate. A few years ago, for example, I discovered in my basement a shoebox filled with old 8 mm films from my childhood, films unseen for decades. For a birthday present, my wife had them transformed into a DVD; and so—for the first time in decades—I watched myself at the age of nine or ten, a young but surprisingly recognizable form of myself. One memorable scene takes place on Christmas morning at my family's home in Connecticut. My sister and I stand at the top of the staircase, looking down into the living room. I begin to wring my hands together, and you can almost hear me cackling. (It's a silent film, of course.) Then the camera follows us down the stairs and pans over to the Christmas tree, its lights blinking ineffectively in the sunshine that flowed through the picture window. The tree looms over an enormous, multicolored pile of loot, ribbons, and paper reflecting the glare of the camera's floodlight. For a moment I stand transfixed, stunned by the vast expanse of gifts. Then I plunge into the pile, ripping off wrapping, glancing quickly at one gift, and moving on to the next, and the next, and the next. After a few minutes, the camera turns to my mother, who's looking down at my sister and me, arms folded, shaking her head. Even in the silence, the message is unmistakable. My mother is stunned (and so am I, in retrospect) at this remarkable expression of greed.

While I may be a bit more subtle nowadays on Christmas morning, the problem remains. All of us need or, more correctly, *want* lots of stuff—whether it's money, electronic doodads, a new car, jewelry, a recreational vehicle, or a cabin in the mountains. Our culture seems to demand that we acquire more and more and more. And so Paul reminds us that we need to reframe our understanding of the world and its resources. God provides enough. He doesn't promise that we'll be rich or that he will fulfill all of our fantasies. There may be much, or there may be little, but it will be sufficient to enable us to follow Jesus. Whatever we do or don't have, the Lord is overwhelmingly generous.

As I write these words, I must be honest that a "yeah, but" is going through my mind. We have all seen painful images on television of starving children, perhaps in the developing world, perhaps in our own country, their bellies distended and their eyes dull and lifeless. How is it possible to talk of God's abundance when so many on our planet face starvation and death? The fourth chapter of Philippians and the images on our TV screens seem to work at horrible cross-purposes. Honesty requires me to take note of the anomaly—and also to recognize that the solution may be in our own hands. Perhaps our own failure to internalize Jesus' words—"Just as you did it to one of the least of these who are members of my family, you did it to me" (Matthew 25:40)—and to live them out is at the heart of our planet's inability to sustain its human creatures. We will probably never, in this life, be able either to understand or to correct the overwhelming disparity between the rich or the poor. But Paul's reminder about God's abundance can offer us an incentive to action and a challenge that discipleship involves (among other things) attention to the suffering world around us.

Second, Paul asks his friends in Philippi to remember that they themselves have been generous. "In any case," Paul says, "it was good of you to share my distress" (4:14). Paul uses a strong word here. When he talks about his distress (the Greek word is *thlipsis*, which refers to a kind of relentless pressure), he's recognizing the fact that the Philippian Christians have voluntarily identified themselves with Paul's apostolic trials. How have they done that? "You Philippians indeed know that in the early days of the gospel, when I left Macedonia, no church shared with me in the matter of giving and receiving except you alone. For even when I was in Thessalonica, you sent me help for my needs more than once. Not that I seek the gift, but I seek the profit that accumulates to your account" (4:15–17). The Philippians have been regular contributors in support of Paul's ministry, virtually from the start of their association. (When Paul left Philippi, his next stop was Thessalonica, Acts 16:40–17:1; and so his reference to that city indicates that the Philippians' generosity began immediately after Paul's departure.) In accepting these gifts, Paul violated his own policy. He was a tentmaker by trade (Acts 18:3), and typically he worked with his hands to provide for his ministry's needs. At the height of his conflict with the church in Corinth, he asserts proudly, "I proclaimed God's good news to you free of charge" (2 Corinthians 11:7). But there was something unique about his relationship with the church in Philippi, and so he set aside standard practice and accepted their gifts. Now, with Paul in prison, the Philippians have renewed their financial support, and Paul is overwhelmed by their ongoing generosity.

While the relationship between Paul and the Philippian Christians may have been unique, the congregation's makeup was far from unusual. The Philippian church was typical of Paul's newly planted congregations—a mixed community of Jews and Gentiles, with a few rich members (e.g., Lydia; see Acts 16:14) and a large number of people on the financial margins of society. We're not told specifically about the slave and free ratio in Philippi, but the congregation would inevitably have included people in bondage. In other words, whatever motivated Paul to violate his "no financial support" policy, it wasn't the Philippians's wealth. Perhaps the very warmth (as we explored in Chapter 1) that drew Paul and his friends in Philippi together provided all the reason he needed to say yes to their offer of financial support. Shared affection led to shared resources.

I will never forget my visit to Jan's chicken coop. Following a Sunday morning Eucharist with one of the larger parishes in the diocese, the priest invited me to join him in bringing Holy Communion to Jan, a parish shut-in. On the way, Father Bruce told me to brace myself for Jan's housing: she lives, he said, in a chicken coop. My first reaction was incredulity. How could such a thing be, in an upper-middle class congregation? As we drove up the lane leading to the house, corn rising on each side and forming something of a living tunnel, I became a believer. Jan met us at the door and ushered us into . . . the chicken coop. The building had been insulated, blessedly, to protect Jan from the challenging Northern Indiana winters, and rudimentary plumbing and electrical outlets had been added. But her home had unmistakably begun its life as a chicken coop, now upgraded and marginally habitable. Chickens, of course, do not require much personal space. Human beings do. Jan and her possessions were jammed into a small, hut-like structure that barely gave us room to turn around. What overwhelmed me, however, was not her poverty but her generosity. She welcomed us as lavishly as she was able, spread out tea and cookies, and made us as comfortable as the setting allowed. I discovered that Jan was something of a mentor to students at a local Christian college. Every week, collegians make their way to the chicken coop, to be entertained and encouraged and challenged. Young people learn generosity from the poorest of the poor. Jan is a mighty woman of God: poor and generous at once, with an enormous heart and an outgoing spirit. She reminds me of Paul's friends in Philippi.

In the end, Paul accepts the Philippians' gifts not because he needs the money, but because these Christians need to give. "The profit . . . accumulates to your account" (4:17). It's in their best interests and ours to be generous. Giving unconditionally—writing Jesus a blank check— is at the heart of the Christian life. This biblical principle may be a helpful corrective to a mistake that churches often make at "stewardship time." ("Stewardship" is the term that Christians often apply to the concept of giving. We are all stewards, managers, of God's bounty. Everything belongs to him: our time, our gifts and talents, and our resources. Our job is to take care of this bounty, to use it for his glory.) Typically, when the "fall campaign" arrives and church leaders ask parishioners to make a pledge for the coming year, they do so by presenting a tentative budget. If you give, they imply, we can put on a new roof, inaugurate a nifty youth program, heat the church comfortably in the winter, and make a down payment on that long-awaited pipe organ. In other words, we ask people to pledge to their own self-interest.

Paul's approach is quite different. He tells his Philippian friends that giving is good for them, not the result of giving, but giving itself. That's a radical idea, indeed. Neither Paul nor God needs their money. Paul knows from his own experience that the Lord has always taken care of him. But the Philippians, for their souls' sake, have discovered the grace of generosity, and it has transformed their lives. They need to give.

Third, Paul tells his friends that giving is a sign of something much, much deeper than the gift itself. "I have been paid in full," he says, "and have more than enough; I am fully satisfied, now that I have received from Epaphroditus the gifts you sent, a fragrant offering, a sacrifice acceptable and pleasing God. And my God will fully satisfy every need of yours according to his riches in glory in Christ Jesus" (4:18–19). At this point Paul imports a concept from the Old Testament. Ancient Israelite worship was rather grittier than ours. They offered God not only prayer and praise and song, but animals—sometimes in thanksgiving, sometimes in reparation for their sins. "The life of the flesh is in the blood," Moses told the Israelites, "and I have given it to you for making atonement for your lives on the altar" (Leviticus 17:11). Once sacrificed, the remains were burned. "Then the priest shall turn the whole into smoke on the altar as a burnt offering, an offering by fire of pleasing odor to the Lord" (Leviticus 1:9). The symbolism, while difficult to modern sensibilities, is powerful. Smoke rises. The Lord smells it. He likes what he smells. That, says Paul, is what we're doing when we make our resources available to the Lord. It's our equivalent of the fragrant offering. We're giving God our very best, making it available to him. God likes what he smells.

If you want to know people's real priorities, a friend once told me, look in two places: their date book and their checkbook. Where you invest your time and your money is the best indication of where you invest your life. "For where your treasure is," Jesus tells his disciples, "there your heart will be also" (Matthew 6:21). God rejoices in hearts and minds and resources freely made available to him. Even the most ordinary gift offered to the Lord—a check in the plate on Sunday morning, time spent with a difficult but spiritually open neighbor, muscle power employed hammering nails at a Habitat for Humanity project—warms the divine heart. God likes what he smells.

Years ago, during my first mission trip to Uganda, our team stopped for a few days in Nairobi, Kenya, before making the short flight to Entebbe. We wanted to get ourselves onto East African time and arrive in Uganda as rested as possible. Since our Nairobi stopover included a Sunday, we attended a Swahili service at St. Stephen's Church in the Joro'o district. The liturgy itself, of course, was incomprehensible, but I could recognize the basic Anglican shape and elements. Swahili, on the other hand, is a wonderfully phonetic language. Although I couldn't understand the words, I sang enthusiastically, "Bwana Jesu, naja naja," the refrain in the Swahili version of "Just As I Am." The offertory may have been the most universal segment of the service, with this exception: instead of plates being passed up and down the aisle, American fashion, the congregation left their pews and moved forward to present gifts of money. I say "moved forward," but that doesn't quite capture it. They *danced* forward. I joined them, albeit awkwardly. We moved toward the altar, bodies swaying, drums beating in time to the music, and dropped our gifts into large woven baskets. It felt, for the very first time in my life, as though I was, in fact, offering myself. Paul's words of encouragement to the Roman Christians—"present your bodies to the Lord as a living sacrifice, holy and acceptable to God" (Romans

12:1)—took on literal meaning as my money and my body became one in self-giving. That's the deeper reality that Paul highlights when he calls the Philippians' gift "a fragrant offering, a sacrifice acceptable and pleasing to God" (4:19). God likes what he smells when we yield ourselves to him, when we make ourselves unconditionally available to Jesus.

Paul concludes with doxology, a word of praise that is the ultimate expression of joy. "To our God and Father be glory forever and ever. Amen" (4:20). In the end, joy isn't about what we feel. That's beyond our control, and if we scrunch our eyebrows together and try to make ourselves feel joyful, we will inevitably fail. Paul offers us another way. He invites his friends in Philippi and he invites us to say yes to Jesus, to give ourselves without reservation to the King of kings, and thus to glorify God—Father, Son, and Holy Spirit—from whom all blessings flow.

QUESTIONS FOR REFLECTION

1. Can you think of a time when God provided for your needs when you least expected it? How, in doing so, did he surprise you?

2. What new expression of generosity may be God's invitation to you today? How is he stretching you to give?

3. How have others been generous to you?

4. How is Jesus asking you to "dance" your way into new and deeper discipleship?